Blackwell

The Badger War Lord

Book One

Blackwell

The Badger War Lord Book One

Marlon Birch

Birch Tree Publishing

The Badger War Lord

Book One:

I dedicate The Badger War Lord to my Son Kai Birch, my Grandparents Francis and Claris Birch, my cousin Camille. Along with never ending love towards Mr.&Mrs. Christie and Kiri for without them none of these books would've been written.

Chapter 1

The late summer afternoon sun glinted off the greaves and breastplate of his battle attire as the mighty badger stood in the road before the giant brown-brick fortress. For fifteen seasons Dun Scotus had followed the footsteps of fate, and now that path had led him here. The paw of destiny was close, and soon he would know whether all his efforts would be enough to ensure the safety of his lands. No beast of late had appeared too great a challenge for him. Dun Scotus's fixed gaze traveled from the crenellated battlements atop the perimeter wall to the heavy double doors of the main gate to the bell tower which reared against the sky, and the peaks of the main fortress building which reached twice as high the badger's trained warrior's eye however, missed no detail.

This, is truly a place of great strength, a fortress to withstand any siege or assault thrown against it. No wonder it was renowned far and wide as a place of sanctuary in times of trouble and need. Except, now their watchfulness left something to be desired. He had been standing outside their gate for some time, apparently unnoticed. Occasionally his ears caught some snatches of noise from within, some shout or song or mirthful laugh. Perhaps he'd arrived here on a day of celebration, when their guard was lowered and their minds attuned to more frivolous matters. Their reputation for food, drink and festivity was as famous as their hospitality.

No matter, he was no thieving villain seeking to slip into their midst to cause mischief and mayhem. Where Dun Scotus went, all would know. Inhaling and filling his lungs and swelling his chest to the limits of his armor casing, he reared back his head and unleashed a thunderous cry that reverberated throughout the surrounding countryside of Primley.

"Blackwellllllllllllll!" Dun Scotus roared.

Immediately, all sounds from inside the walls were silenced, and within moments heads started to appear along the top of the western wall. In very short-order the battlements were packed with bodies, as countless elves, horses, deers, mice, and squirrels peered warily over the brown brickwork to see what manner of creature had interrupted their revelries with such a cry. Every gaze was locked upon him, and a sense of expectancy filled the air as the woodlanders and warrior faced each other in silence. Finally the silence was broken by an older mouse in an ornate habit, brightly multi-colored. "Greetings!" he called down from the wall top. "Are you in need of assistance of some kind beast?"

"Are you the Lord, or Father?" Dun Scotus shouted back. "Yes … er, no … "

Dun Scotus's lip curled in bemusement. "Well, which is it then? And be quick about it" The old mouse said. "My name is Brae, the acting counsel of Blackwell" "Good. Then, my mission concerns you as well, and any other creature of authority and fighting stead who dwells within your walls.

I am Lord Dun Scotus of Astapailia, I bear urgent tidings. It is vital that I speak with all of Blackwell's leaders. Let me in please. "Half the faces disappeared from the battlements then, as a delegation descended to open the gated main entrance to Blackwell Fortress. This still left a large contingent of Blackwell creatures up above, not wanting to tear their eyes away from the armored badger, not even for a moment. It was not every day that one of the legendary Badger Lords of Astapailia came to visit Primley woods. The labored scraping of wood against wood rent the air as the main bolt was slid back, and one side of the double door swung open. In the shadows beyond Dun Scotus you could see two adult mice, a male in a white habit and a female in a yellow one. Along with a large female horse clad in a simple sack cloth smock. A female mouse stepped forward.

"I am Lady Brae, and this is brother Skara, our Blackwell recorder and historian. Also," she indicated the larger creature just behind her, "is Neo, our Blackwell Badger Mother. Welcome to Blackwell. Are you alone, Lord?" "Yes, for now. I have troops far to the south, but they are presently engaged."

"Oh? Is there trouble there?"

"I have come to tell of great happenings in the lands, both good and evil. There is much to speak of, and it cannot all be said out here standing in the road."

The Blackwell-dwellers regarded Dun Scotus uncertainly for a few moments. He was quite openly armed, and armed very well, in the fashion of all warriors. Burnished silver armor encased his upper body from neck to waist. His hind legs were like tree trunks, with battle scars showing here and there through the gray-brown fur.

He carried no helmet, but the back piece of his steel suit rose in a flange like a high collar, shielding most of the back of his head. The circular shield and axe strapped across his back both looked to have seen many a battle, and a great sword hung sheathed at his side. If this is an evil-minded creature, he could obviously cause untold harm once admitted into the walls Blackwell. However, the Badger Lords of Astapailia were known far and wide for their courage, honesty and nobility.

They were the perennial protectors of the coast-lands from the weasel and pirate hordes. Dun Scotus stood before them, proud, head high, his earnest gaze meeting each of theirs unflinchingly.

Lady Brae stirred herself as if from a trance. "Forgive us, Lord, but we are unaccustomed to receiving one so great as yourself. My apologies if we gave the appearance of rudeness or mistrust. You have come to us on a day of celebration, and you are more than welcome to join us." She looked over her shoulder, where others had gathered in the entrance way behind Neo. "Clear the way! Make room for Lord Dun Scotus to pass! "The Blackwellers retreated, and the three Blackwell leaders led Dun Scotus through the gate into Blackwell. The protective wall which encircled the fortress and its grounds was of such thickness that passing under it was almost like passing through a massive tunnel.

The other side of the gate gave way to the meticulously cared-for greens ward of the inner lawns. By this time most of the onlookers up top had made their way down the wall stairs to join with the other revelers from the fortress grounds, and the gathering around the newly-arrived War-Lord was quite large. Many were infants and young ones, peeking through the legs of their parents and guardians or out from behind them. A few of the more precocious ones stood up front with the adults, for a better view. Dun Scotus scanned the Fortress within the high walls. The Fortress proper with its attached bell tower stood tall and proud and looked silver in the sunlight, crafted from the same dusky sand-stone as the protective perimeter wall. Beyond, he could see a large pond and a stand of well-tended trees, probably a fruit orchard. The plain natural beauty of the place stirred his heart, but the practical utility appealed to his warrior side. With its own food and water supply within the sealed grounds, Blackwell was designed as much as a fortress as it was a place of peace and refuge he thought. Between the main gate and the pond, a large baking pit had been dug, and set up near it were many tables spread with a multitude of delicacies to make any beast's mouth water.

Savory aromas of many kinds hung in the air, mingling with the mellow burning odor of the hot charcoal in the pit below. An Ox came from behind Dun Scotus to see, to the closing of the main gate. While Abbest Brae invited him to partake of the feast displayed before them. "We are celebrating the elevation of our chief Stag here to the official position of Skipper of all Blackwell's Armies. You must be tired and hungry after your travels. Please join us at our tables, and later we can discuss the matters which have brought you to Blackwell."

"If it is all the same," said Dun Scotus, "I would rather get right to the business at paw. I can see your tables are well stocked, and I am sure there will be plenty left after we have spoken."

Brother Skara snorted a loud laugh! "You might not say that so quickly, if you'd ever seen our newly-appointed Gorver Skippy Belly-empty in action. He's the champion eater at Blackwell, and when he's around, food usually isn't. Well, not for long, any-way.

A snort of another kind sounded behind them. Dun Scotus turned to see the Stag who'd gone to close the gates. "I'll have you know it's hard work keeping all O me Stag crew well-drilled an' in proper muscular shape. A beast's gotta keep himself well energized for such a job." The Stag turned from Brother Skara to Dun Scotus and gave an informal bow. "Right honored to meet ya, Ma'Lord." Dun Scotus regarded the brawny Stag. "If you are Blackwell's Skipper of Otters, you will want to be at this meeting." He turned to Lady of Blackwell. "As will every Blackwell who holds a position of decision making or defense. It distresses me to pull you good folk from your feast, but these matters are of utmost importance."

"They must be serious indeed, for you to urge such haste." Abbest Brae turned to Gorver. "Round up the other chief Blackwell leaders, our High King is not here at the moment so we act in his stead. Terious, Terkmore, Strongwing, any other beast you think should be at this meeting. Brother Skara and I will show Lord Dun Scotus down to the Great Hall. We'll meet you all down there."

The Stag saluted smartly and hurried off to obey. Abbest Brae scanned the crowd until she saw Abbot Graupulous, who'd come down from the wall top where he'd been the first to greet the Badger Lord. He wasn't hard to spot in his fancy embroidered robe. Staying on the fringes of the gathering, the old mouse seemed very self-conscious about his manner of dress, and hesitated when lady Brae called him over to him. "You heard all of that, Graupulous?" He nodded. "Indeed I did. Although I scarcely know what to make of it all."

"Nor do I. I've only been Lady of Blackwell for a short time. You should be at this meeting too. You, have many seasons of experience, and I would not be witout your counsel now. "The old mouse nodded once. "Of all the times for you and sister Juliett to bully me into wearing a multicolored clown's outfit, it would be the day that a Badger Lord visit!" He gave a sheepish grin toward Lord Dun Scotus. "You must forgive me, My Lord. Normally, , I am not dressed like this.

"Do not concern yourself, Lord. There are more important matters to concern us than your choice of garment on this day. Abbest Brae is right; you most certainly should join us."

"Then I most certainly will."

The assembled Blackwellers stood and watched their old Father Graupulous and young abbest Brae escort the mysterious, armored badger into their stronghold.

After all of Blackwell's chief leaders and defenders had gone down to the hastily-called council in the Great Hall, the rest of the Blackwell-dwellers were left to talk amongst themselves up on the festival grounds.

There was much speculation on the significance of the badger's unexpected arrival. Some beasts returned to the tables, where much food from the feast remained, and expressed their opinions through stuffed cheeks and chewing jaws. Most, however, had eaten their fill and chose to relax in small scattered groups on the greensward or at the pond's edge, dabbling their paws to relieve the summer heat. But no matter where they congregated, no tongue was still.

In the shade of the orchard, three friends joined in the speculation. The two young mouse brothers, Syril and Serius, sat with their constant mole friend Rufus, beneath a damson tree whose fruit hung small in the early season.

"What a bloody Badger Lord!" Serius said, still amazed by the sight of Dun Scotus. "He must have been twice the size of our badger."

"Hurr, they 'were more like like three times, burr hurr," Rufus said through a mouthful of unripe damson. "An' that armor ...what a powerful beast!"

Syril, the oldest of the three, had a faraway look in his eye. "They said he's from Astapailia ... a Badger Lord of the Mountains."

Serius looked up at his brother. "Astapailawottawho?"

"Astapailia," Syril corrected. "You remember, Brother Skara gave a lesson on it once."

"Yurr, et be a gurt and mighty place boi western sea," added Rufus, wiping damson juice from his chin with a digging claw.

"The Badger Lords have been masters of the mountain fortress for ... well, as long as any beast can remember. They've always protected the coast lands from searat invasions, giving us here in Primley country peace from pirate raiders and slavers." Syril turned upon the grass where he sat, commanding the attention of his sibling and mole-friend. "Legend has it that Astapailia was a volcano once, when the world was much younger than it is now. I have heard that the very first Badger Lords were born from the fires of the mountain, and they tamed that same fire for their mighty forges.

No creature commands flame and hammer and anvil like they do. Well, that's because they were born in fire."

"Hurr hurr, don't you'd be berleevin' that, Serius," Rufus laughed. "They'm be jus' fairy stories, fer infants an' such."

"Don't be too sure, Rufus," Cyril said to the mole. "The sword of Blackwell's founder Septimus the Warrior was made by one of the Badger Lords of Astapailia. That weapon is older than the Abbey itself, and its blade is still as keen as the day it was forged." "Burr, there'm be lots o legend surrounding ee sword o Septimus," Rufus nodded. "Sum-beasts says et were made o' metal wot fell from outen ee skoi."

Serius's eyes went wide. "Metal from the sky!" he whispered.

"Cudd be, fer all oi knows. But foxes be foxes, an' no beast be a-borned frum foire."

"Oh, you've got no imagination, Rufus!" Syril chided. "Sometimes I think you moles are too sensible for your own good."

"Senzurble enuff not to go getting mixed up in war an' such, loik you'm mousefolk." Rufus rummaged through a pouch at his waist. "Any beast care fer summ carndied chesknutters?"

The two mice ignored his offer of sweets. "What did you suppose that Badger Lord wants with us here at Blackwell?" Serius asked his companions.

"We'll find out soon enough, when the meeting in the Great Hall lets out." Cawnor cast an envious glance toward the Abbey building. "Wish I could be down there, though. Hear it with my own ears. Adults never tell us young ones everything that goes on. If, that badger is here on an errand of war, you can bet we will never get to hear the good stuff."

"Gudd stuff?" Rufus shook his head. "Bain't nuthin' gudd about war, Serius. Oi'm surprised at you'm speakin' suchloik. Wot'd Brudder Brehon say if'n 'ee was to 'ear you making glory talk about war?"

"He won't find out, unless you go blabbing it to him, mole."

Rufus clutched at his round stomach. "Urr ... oi think they damsons doan't be roipe enuff for proper ettin'. Moi tummee feels sick."

Syril regarded his friend. "I take back what I said about moles being so sensible."

Nine creatures sat around the big table in the Great Hall.

Dun Scotus was given the head seat, both as a place of honor and because he would presumably be doing most of the talking. Abbest Brae seated herself at the Badger Lord's right paw.

Lady Brae made the introductions. "You've already met Brother Skara, our Blackwell recorder and historian ... Father Graupulous...Neo, our badger ... and Gorver, our newly-elevated Skipper of Stags. That squirrel next to Gorver is Vondick, chief of the Primley Woods Partrol. Between him and Neo, You will see our Terkmore. Also, that sparrow between Skara and Strongwing is, the leader of the sparrow-folk,who dwell in our attic spaces."

The bird, who sat upon a special low perch that enabled him to sit at a level appropriate to the table, bowed his head to the badger. "We did not meet earlier, My Lord, for my beak was stuck in a pot of flan when you arrived. Not my most dignified moment, I'm afraid."

"So there you have it," Abbest Brae concluded. "Together, I suppose you could say we make up the leadership of Blackwell Abbey."

Dun Scotus nodded slowly. "Fine, fine."

The badger's deep voice echoed off the stone walls and the rafters over head. The Great Hall was an enormous space, large enough to hold the entire Abbey population, as it had during many past celebrations, and on many a fierce winter's night when the gusting cold had penetrated the upper dormitories. The other creatures at the table waited for Dun Scotus to continue, but the warrior remained silent as the echoes faded. As the silence threatened to become awkward, Abbest Brae broke it.

"It has been many generations since the last contact between Blackwell and Astapailia.

How is it that a Badger Lord of the Mountain comes to be wandering Primley Woods, all alone?"

"I have wandered much farther than this," Dun Scotus said. "For the past fifteen seasons my brother Nantrom has held the Lordship of Astapailia, while I have journeyed far and wide on matters of concern to us both."

"Two Badger Lords?" Brother Skara remarked. "I do not believe I have ever heard of a time when there were two Lords of the Mountain, and I know the histories very well."

"We took joint Lordship of Astapailia while we were still quite young. I am the elder, but we always ruled as equals. It is good that there are two of us, for these are times for warriors."

Lady Brae looked to the Badger Lord with great concern. "You have spoken of nothing but graveness and urgency since you arrived at our gate, My Lord. Tell us what weighs upon you so, and what it has to do with Blackwell."

"It is a matter of prophecy," Dun Scotus began. "High in the upper reaches of Astapailia there is a chamber which has served as both tomb and throne room over the generations. Carved into its rock walls can be found the living history of all that has come before, and hints at what may yet be. You see, there come times when we Badger Lords are gripped by a mania, a trance, and it is during such times that we go to that chamber, and fate will speak through us into the rock. We awake as if from a dream-less sleep to see what we have carved, for we have no awareness while in the trance. Many prophecies have been fore told in this manner, and more than one Lord of the Mountain has read his doom in words carved by his own paw. It is not always easy to bear this burden of destiny, but it is our lot and we accept it."

"Yes, I have heard of this phenomenon, " said Skara. "Septimus the Warrior, our founder, visited Astapailia during the Great Battle, and his sword was forged by one of your distant predecessors, Mac Alpine the Fighter and Rouge were two Badger Lords who visited Blackwell early in its history, and one of our early fox mother Orva, I believe spent much of her childhood in the mountain. More recently, Lady Clara was a former ruler of Astapailia who became our fox matriarch. There is much in our histories about that legendary place."

"You know your history very well," Dun Scotus commended Skara. "Fifteen seasons ago, I was seized by such a mood as I have described.

For the better part of a day, I was in the trance, adding to the carvings on the chamber walls. When I finally came to my senses and looked upon what I had writen, I was filled with dread. It was a great prophecy, and an evil one." Every face at the table was grave, every gaze locked upon Dun Scotus like iron.

"What did it say?" Lady Brae ventured. "That a time of unmatched crisis will come in our lifetimes. That it will encompass all the lands, and all of its creatures."

"War?" breathed old Father Graupulous.

"War as never before."

An icy claw seemed to reach through the ceiling to clutch at the very heart of the Great Hall, as the breath of doom hung upon the still air.

"Tell us," Lady Brae implored, "exactly what does this prophecy say?"

"It is vague about the exact shape of the threat, "Dun Scotus explained. "It seems to suggest more a continued state of turmoil or chaos, rather than any single battle, war or enemy. It may be a time of many different armies facing each other in a multitude of places, over the course of seasons. One thing is clear: the long peace which has held sway over Primley Woods is soon to end."

"It is no wonder that you appear so grim," said Lady Brae, the color drained from her face. "So, what is to be done?" "After reading this prophecy, I left Astapailia in the care of my brother Nantrom and the brave fighting stags of the Mega Patrol who served the Badger Lords well. They have held the lands along the western coast secure. "While my brother guarded the mountain and the coast-lands, I wandered far and wide throughout the lands, from the base of the great south cliff wall to the far north, all the way to the shore of the eastern sea where the lands narrow. Always I was vigilant for any hint or clue of the coming storm, always assessing the mood of the creatures I met to know whether they could be counted as friend or foe in time of crisis. I am preparing.

For you see," Dun Scotus leaned his armored bulk farther over the table toward them, "I am not wholly convinced that the prophecy is inevitable. It may just be that, if we tread upon the knife edge of fate and choose our course of action most carefully, we may be able to deny this destiny. Even if we cannot, measures can be taken to ensure that as many good and honorable creatures as possible can emerge from this unscathed." He leaned back. "Even Blackwell may be at peril when the storm breaks. I am here to assist you in defending your Abbey."

"Defend it from what?" Asked Orva. "How can we know what steps to take if we don't know what's coming?" "Neo has a good point," Father Graupulous said. "Tell us, My Lord, have you seen nothing in all your journeys that would answer this for us?"

"Nothing definite," Dun Scotus answered, "although I can tell you of one development that is most unsettling. The power of the sea-rats has grown great, perhaps greater than ever before. Of all the enemies we may come to face, they pose the most obvious and immediate threat. "At the time that I carved my prophecy and began my wanderings, there were two great sea-rat lords, Utropio and Carnal, and each strove to make himself king over all his kind. But their power was nearly equally balanced, and neither could gain the upper paw over the other.

"The day dawned at last when Utropio and Carnal moved in to open conflict against each other. Carnal was the more competent of the two, and commanded the loyalty of his captains and crew, while Utropio was more treacherous and cruel. Utropio slew Carnal and prepared to make himself king of all the sea-rats. But providence was not kind to him, for in my journeys I spent some time of my own at sea, and fate placed me close at paw when these events unfolded. I slew Utropio, recognizing him for the vile creature he was. This is how it came to pass that the two most powerful of the sea-rats both met their deaths on the same day."

The Blackwellers sat in awed silence at the telling of this tale.

It was Father Graupulous who broke it. "But, if Carnal and Utropio are both dead, where is the sea-rats threat?"

"Utropio and Carnal kept the sea-rats evenly divided," Dun Scotus explained. "On the face of it, their deaths might have seemed a great boon to all good and honest creatures. But it cleared the way for a single Badger Lord to emerge and unite the two fleets. Such a figure has indeed come to power: Jurista, one of Utropio's former captains, who now calls himself Cervantar the Sea-rat King.

He commanded the respect of Utropio's surviving crews, and with Utropio dead, he was able to bring that badger's leaderless horde under his rule as well.

He has sealed the breach, and rebuilt the island fortress of Seraphane. Cervantar is probably the first true Fox King since Skarka of old, only more dangerous. His fleet is vast, his fighters are well-trained, and he has raided shore settlements all up and down the coast ... although so far he has always been careful to land well north and south of Astapailia, beyond the range of my brother's secret patrols. But he harbors ambitions of empire, and his mastery of the sea lanes is absolute. If his power continues to grow, he may soon try to challenge Astapailia directly."

"Then surely," concluded Abbess Brae, "this Cervantar will be the bringer of the great crisis you prophesized?"

Dun Scotus shook his head. "I do not think so. Cervantar's sea power may be uncontested, but his crews are not so accustomed to fighting on land. Even if they were to capture Astapailia and the coast-lands, he would be hard pressed to project his power inland very far. Cervantar is no fool; he will not jeopardize his sea kingdom to take territory beyond the waterways. No, Cervantar is not the only threat to our lands, and he may not even prove to be the worst. I suspect there will be another enemy, perhaps more than one, whose threat we have yet to perceive.

The danger may come from some undiscovered source within these lands, or it may come from without many of the regions east and south of here are strange, and have not felt the paws of honest creatures for many seasons. Other evils of Cervantar's magnitude may lie out there as well, as yet unbeknownst to us."

"And you have no idea what they might be?" the Abbess asked.

"No ... just a feeling that the storm is about to break, and we must gird ourselves for the worst. This is why I have come to Blackwell now. I have spent most of these past seasons up north, and I have slain many evil creatures there, and still that region remains harsh and warlike. I have also assembled allies who will assist us.

My brother and I have always relied upon Blackwell to hold peace and order in Primley. However now I feel I have done all I can for the Northlands, and the time has come to consolidate the power of Blackwell and Astapailia in this region. The two protectors must unite in common cause. Together we will face these troubles, and through our twin strength persevere."

Dun Scotus looked to Brae. "With your permission, Abbess, I would like to take charge of the defenses of this Abbey ... or, at the very least, be appointed as special advisor to your own defenders, so that we may fortify Blackwell against any possible assault. I am a born warrior, and Blackwell is currently without a champion to wield the sword of Septimus. My skills and experience are needed here."

Vondick cleared his throat. Thus far the squirrel had held his tongue, content to listen while the wiser heads of Blackwell conferred with Dun Scotus. But now he spoke up.

"With all due respect, Lord, we've always looked out for ourselves here at Blackwell. Our wall gates have recently been strengthened and renovated. We squirrels of the Primley Patrol range far and wide to scout for enemies, as do Strongwing and his Celtar. Gorver and I regularly drill our defenders. There is a network of fortified tunnels connecting all the most important sites within the Abbey grounds. I really can't see how we can do much more to improve our defenses."

"Me bushy tailed matey's right," Sha put in. "This ol' Abbey's 'bout as shipshape as any beast c'd want her. Don't see as she needs much in the' way o' improving."

Dun Scotus's dispassionate gaze traveled around the crescent of faces, from mouse to mole to otter to badger to sparrow and back again. The Abbess was afraid that Gorver and Terious might have offended him, but when Dun Scotus spoke it was with his typical calm.

"In the time that I stood unnoticed outside your walls, an enemy could have set fire to your main gate and had it burned halfway through. If I had not announced my presence when I did, how much longer would I have had to stand in the road before one of your sentries spotted me?"

Gorver and Terious cleared their throats and uttered a few "ers" and "ums," but they were not the only ones at the table to look down in chagrin.

"Lord Dun Scotus is right," said Abbess Brae. "We Blackwellers have grown accustomed to peace. All of us here have never known anything else. We have lowered our guard in recent seasons, and we should be thankful it was Lord Scotus who pointed this out to us, rather than an enemy. There is a time of crisis coming, and this warrior has offered us the benefit of his knowledge and assistance. It would be both foolish and ungracious of us to turn him away."

She turned to the armored-badger. "We accept your offer of help, My Lord, and gladly welcome any counsel you would share with us."

"There is still much to speak of," said Dun Scotus, "but it can wait for another day. For now I would like to get right to the task of inspecting this Abbey for myself from top to bottom, inside and out, to see how its defenses might be improved. I will need some of you to show me around. Blueprints of Blackwell would also be helpful, if you have such plans. I would like to read any detailed accounts you may have of the wars that you have fought over the seasons."

"Brother Skara can help you with those last two items," Brae said, "since, as you have seen, he knows his history very well. He is in charge of the Abbey archives, and should be able to find what you need."

"I am at your service, My Lord." Skara turned to the Abbess. "I also have another idea, Dranda ... er, Abbess. It strikes me that many times in the past when Blackwell has faced a crisis, our founders seem to have foreseen those troubles and left some bit of hidden wisdom to help get us through. There was the carving under the great tapestry and the clues in Septimus's tomb that led us to rediscover the lost sword of Septimus when we needed it against Teivel the Terrible, and the verse inscribed up on the roof that aided us in the struggle against Walldow and Salga the slaver fox. Maybe they've left something similar for this occasion."

"Good thinkin', Skara matey!" Gorver declared exuberantly. "That's usin' yer ol' brain-box!"

"Yes," agrees the Abbess. "But where will you look?"

"The old records would be as good a place to start as any," Skara said, "starting with the founding of Blackwell and going right up to the present. I could use some help with this since that will be a tremendous amount of reading. Our two young bell-ringers, Syril and Serius, both have a good head for history. Perhaps they could be excused from their usual bell-ringing duties to assist me."

"I think we can find other willing paws to pull the bell ropes for a while," the Abbess assured him. "And of course you yourself will have to be excused from your teaching duties while you're conducting this search of the archives. In times of trouble, sacrifices must be made ... as I'm sure your students will readily agree!"

She stood to signal the end of the council, and the other eight creatures arose as well. "We've come up with some good ideas on where to start. Let us now go and make Blackwell ready and, just let any evil creature try to take it away from us!"

CHAPTER 2

On the banks of the Abbey pond, Grauparus the otter danced about sparring with a young sparrow.

Even though the bird had to hop about on one leg, clutching its stout quarter staff in the other claw, he held his own against Grauparus. It was a fighting style pioneered seasons before by Strongwing, leader of Blackwell's sparrows, and since adopted by many of the bird folk. The rapid fire clacking of the oaken rods resounded in the late afternoon air, mingling with the bird-song and insect buzz from beyond the Abbey walls.

On a nearby bench, sister Juliett the Infirmary keeper and Ularus the hedgehog cellar keeper sat tending some of the Abbey's very youngest children. Juliett was a young mouse-maid herself, only recently appointed to her post by Abbess Brae. She was quick with her knowledge of herb lore and the healing arts, but her bed-side manner was still in need of refinement. Dealing with children was her weakest link. But with Brother Skara and Neo both down at the conference in the Great Hall, the odious task had fallen to her.

"Grauparus!" Juliett called out to the young otter with gathering impatience, "you're supposed to be helping with the little ones! Stop playing around like a soggy pup!"

"Aw, Sister Juliett!" Grauparus replied without breaking stride in his jousting, "I gotta get some practice in, or our new Skip Gorver'll brain me." "I'll brain you first if you don't lend a flipper here whoa!" Juliett was balancing a fidgety, pinching mole on one knee and a recalcitrant hedgehog babe on the other, and getting it from both ends a prickly situation indeed. This was doing little to improve her disposition.

Ularus sat alongside Juliett, a baby vole in her lap. "Oh, let him have his fun, Juls. It is a feast day, after all."

"Right, Ularus, it is a feast day," Juliett said indignantly. "All the more reason why you and I shouldn't have to do all the babysitting chores ourselves. Grauparus, drop that pole and get your rudder over here!"

Grauparus, winking mischievously at his sparrow pal, decided to try a new ploy. "Do you hear something, Rafter matey? A sort of high-pitched, annoying ringing in the ears? Must be from that last smack you snuck in on me ol' noggin."

The Celtar cawed raucously and flapped his wings to maintain his one-legged balance. "Me think you get another smack quick soon. Your Jullymouse getting pretty mad."

"Ha! Jullymouse that's a good one!"Grauparus parried a thrust from his sparrow friend and rapped his javelin playfully across Rafter's beak. "Hey, Jullymouse! How's life on the old folks' bench?"

"I'll Jullymouse you, you rascal, if you don't get over here to lend a paw. You're not too old to spank, just like I used to spank you when you acted up before bedtime. Just keep it up, if you don't believe me!"

"Haha! First, you'll hafta catch me, y liddle mousey thing!"

Juliett turned to Ularus, teeth gritted. "Sometimes he's as bad as his father," she growled, not caring how loudly she spoke.

Grauparus lowered his staff and backed out of the dual with Rafter. "Hey, there's no call fer that," he said petulantly. "Leave me ol' Dad outta this, okay?"

"I don't have to leave him out of anything he does a good job of that all by himself. He could at least have shown up for Gorver's promotion ceremony today, but he's off gallivanting in some distant reach of Primley. Rather, be wandering about on his own than here with his only son."

"Easy, now, Sister Ularus told the mouse-maid somewhat crossly. "That was un-necessary."The stout hedgehog adroitly set her bank-vole down on the ground, plucked the troublesome mole-babe from Juliett's lap and passed it to Grauparus, who accepted it without complaint. Within moments the infant was settled down into the otter's brawny arms. Ularus turned back to Juliett. "See? You just gotta know how to handle them!"

As Lord Scotus and the Abbey elders came up the stairs from their Great Hall, the badger warrior paused on the top step to take in the space before him.

The afternoon sun sent its rays through the tall stained glass windows high up on the western wall, spilling vivid multi colors across the red sandstone floor at the far end of the Great Hall and creeping slowly up the opposite wall. Eventually these rainbow-hued beams from one set of windows would meet the frosted panes of their east-facing counterparts. It was a daily summer display that Blackwellers had been enjoying for generations.

"What is it, My Lord?" Abbess Brae asked, her softly spoken words hushed in the face of the Great Hall's cathedral immensity.

"I noticed something earlier, when we were going down to the council. I would like to take a closer look at it." With several of the others following him, he strode over to stand before the tapestry which hung upon one wall.

The ancient tapestry was the Abbey's most prized treasure, dating back to the earliest periods of Blackwell's history. A woven image of Septimus the Warrior, Blackwell's founding champion, adorned the lower edge of the work, which was the oldest part of the tapestry. Succeeding generations had added to it, making this decoration far more than mere art: visitors to the Great Hall could take in at a glance many key chapters in Blackwell's story, boldly embroidered for all to see a fluttering, beautiful chronicle of colored fabric. But for all the additions and all the seasons represented, it was still the visage of Septimus, resplendent with his sword and shield that dominated the tapestry and drew the eye to it before all else.

Brother Skara waved a paw toward the figure and began to explain, "That's Septimus the Warrior, our founding "..........

"Yes, I know," Dun Scotus interrupted, shifting his attention to the items that hung on the wall alongside the tapestry. "And this is his shield and sword?"

"Er, yes," Skara nodded, slightly flustered at having the historical lecture he'd been preparing in his mind cut off so abruptly. "They were both lost for many generations, then rediscovered in the time of Maximus, our second great Warrior. Ever since, they have been cherished and kept well, as reminders of our history and in case we ever need them again."

"But Blackwell currently has no champion to carry the sword of Septimus?"

"No," answered Abbess Brae. "We haven't had one since before I was born. There has been peace in Primley for many, many seasons. We've had no need of a champion."

"Do you mind if I take a closer look?" Dun Scotus asked, reaching out to take the splendid weapon down from its brackets. Testing the balance in his paw (it was a bit small for him, having been made for a mouse, after all), he ran both his gaze and his pawtip up and down the keen edge of the blade, then inspected the handle and pommel stone.

"Yes, a fine weapon indeed," he declared at length. "I forged a sword very similar to this one. I gave it to the captain of my guard in the Northlands, who carries it still."

"That is not too surprising," said Skara, "since this blade was crafted by a Badger Lord such as yourself."

"True." He replaced the sword in its holder, noticing the worn old sandal that hung from one backet. "May I ask what this is doing here?" Dun Scotus inquired, indicating the battered old article of footpaw wear.

Skara, Brae and several of the others grinned and chuckled. But it was the sparrow Strongwing who answered.

"Before she was our Abbess, or even our Infirmary keeper, Brae was a brave and fearless warrior herself. She once used that very same sandal to beat off some of my kin-folk who sought to slay me. I owe my life to her, and to that old shoe."

Dun Scotus shook his head. "So many stories in this place ... I fear I could dwell here for seasons and still not know them all. I will have to spend a great deal of time indeed reading through your histories."

"You will have them tomorrow, My Lord," Skara assured him.

Most of the group started for the door leading to the lawns outside, but Gorver the otter lingered by the sword and shield of Septimus. His longtime squirrel friend Vondick stayed by his side. "What, Gorver?"

After several seconds of regarding the armaments, Gorver lifted down sword, scabbard and belt and fastened them around his waist.

"What do you think you're doing?" Terious asked.

"Well, you 'eard wot that badger said down there," Gorver said. "Tough times a-comin' Blackwell's gonna need a champion soon. Might's well be me."

23

Vondick gave his old companion a smirk. "What makes you think I'm not more entitled to it than you are?"

"Aw, don't be silly, Terious matey your head o th' Forest Patrol. Bow an' arrows're your weapons o choice. 'Sides, I can't think of a better way t celebrate my promotion to Skipper. This's my day, y'know!"

The crowd around the pond's banks grew as the afternoon wore on. The mouse brothers Syril and Serius and their molefriend Rufus came to cool their paws in the inviting waters, as did Friar Calgarus. Speculation about Lord Scotus continued unabated.

"Can't be good, a beast like that coming to us out of the blue all of a sudden," the old mouse cook shook his head in consternation. "Calling all our leaders down into a council like that ... no news is good news, and that badger looked like he was brimming with news."

"Oh, don't be such a doom-monger," Ularus chided him. "There's nothing that Blackwell can't handle, if it comes right down to it."

"Well, we're about to find out," said young Grauparus. "Here they all come now. The meeting must be over."

While Abbess Brae and most of the other Abbey leaders showed Lord Scotus to the tables, pointing the badger through the feast leftovers, Gorver grabbed up a vegetable pastie in one paw and a raspberry tart in the other and sauntered over to the group by the pond, the newly-acquired sword of Septimus slapping against his flank in its scabbard as he walked. Blackwell's new Skipper of otters grinned at Grauparus, who stood with the slumbering mole-babe still cradled in his embrace. "Gotcha doin' nurse maid duties now, Grauparus matey?"

Grauparus grinned in return. "I was doin' my drillin' with Rafter here, sir, but Sister Juliett bullied me into lookin' after this mole."

Gorver looked askance at the Infirmary keeper. "You have been bullyin' me star pupil? Shame on ye, marm! Mmph, scrkmph!" He paused to demolish the pastie. "'ave you no shame?"

"The scamp was supposed to be lending a paw with these young ones," Juliett snapped. "Don't you go defending him! Then, he will never take his responsibilities seriously."

"I'd say drillin's a good chunk o his Abbey 'sponsibilities. An' so's knowin' alla his Blackwell's history, and he's good at both o those. Wink 'ere's better at book learnin' than any otter I know. Could be th' first otter Abbot Blackwell ever has."

Grauparus blushed. What Gorver had said was true, but Grauparus was a modest beast, and wasn't accustomed to having praise heaped upon him.

"And I reckon he will have due cause to practice both 'is strengths in th' days ahead, if'n there's anything to what that badger had t say."

This remark grabbed the attention of the Blackwellers there. "What is it, Gorver?" Ularus asked. "What did Lord Dun Scotus tell you down there?"

"Yes," said Juliett, "and why are you wearing the sword of Septimus?"

"Rough seas ahead," Gorver said, making the fruit pastry vanish in one admirable swallow. "Mmrph. Tough times, an' all that."

"Yes, but ... what does that mean? What's going to happen?"

"Well, er ..." Gorver was never a beast to be at a loss for words. But now that he'd been pressed and made to think about it, he realized that, for all Dun Scotus had spoken at the council, he still had no clear idea of just what the coming threat to Blackwell was.

"Can't rightly say," he ventured at last. "Sea-rat kings and prophecies carved in stone ... all a throw beyond a simple waterdog like me, y'know. But that big ol' badger's gonna help us get ready fer it, wotever it is."

"You, sir, are a ninny," Sister Juliett announced. "Here comes Vondick. Maybe that sensible squirrel can give us some real answers."

Blackwell's chief of the Primley Patrol drew up alongside Gorver. He seemed taken off guard by all the expectant gazes that were fixed upon him. "What, did I forget to bathe today?" the hearty squirrel joked.

"We're waiting to hear what happened down there," said Sister Juliett. "This rudder-tailed buffoon can't tell us anything."

"Yes, what can you tell us about that meeting?" echoed Ularus.

Although Vondick was far more earnest and less flamboyant in his speech than Graupuss was, it soon became clear that he was equally at a loss to explain the details of Dun Scotus's prophecy.

"But Skara has an idea," he concluded. "He thinks there might be some clue buried in Blackwell's history that might be able to help us." Terious turned to the two young mouse brothers. "Syril, Serius... Skara would like to have a word with the two of you. He wants you to help him search through the archives. Said you had good heads for this kind of thing."

The two brothers were not overjoyed by the prospect of spending hours or days of this glorious summer in the dingy, dark archive cellars. "But we're the bellringers!" Syril protested.

Gorver reprimanded them sharply. "I'll jerk those waterlogged bellropes meself if that's wot our dear ol' Abbess wants. We all hafta do our part fer th' safety o' this grand ol' place. If you two are needed by me ol' mate Skara, by me rudder that's where you will go!"

Grauparus decided to step in to soften the older otter's scolding. He knew Serius in particular held a respectful fascination for Blackwell's founding mouse warrior.

"You know, if Septimus the Warrior were here, and he thought he could help Blackwell by helping Skara go through the records, he'd consider it his honor-bound warrior's duty to do so. In fact, I'll bet he would have jumped at the chance."

Syril perked up. "Do You really think so?"

"Sure," Vondick chimed in. "And I'll tell you something else. Blackwell's history is full of wars and battles and adventures and quests and mysteries. Reading through it will be like a thousand great bedtime stories all rolled into one. Why, I'd give my prize tail bracelet for the chance at what you've been asked to do. Unfortunately, I'll be needed elsewhere. My tough luck, I guess."

Syril and Serius brightened considerably. They hadn't thought about it like that. "Now you two run along," Vondick prompted them. "Brother Skara is waiting for you." The two mice rushed to obey the squirrel chief, their green novice's habits flapping as they ran.

"That did the trick," Grauparus chuckled.

"Like I said before," Ularus told Juliett with admiration, "you just gotta know how to handle the young ones."

Gorver turned to his young protege. "Hope y'really feel like y' said, Graup, 'cos I promised Skara you'd help out too. Yer head fer Blackwell history's better'n those two put t'gether."

Grauparus's face fell. "But ... but ... "

"Not but's 'bout it, Graup lad," Graupuss said, stepping over to the younger otter and relieving him of the sleeping molebabe. "Off y'go now, Skara's waitin' fer you!"

The sun had nearly set below the western wall when the Abbey leaders emerged from the Great Hall after their meeting with Dun Scotus, and most of Abbey grounds were covered in lengthening shadows. While Abbess Brae showed the badger warrior to the tables, and Gorver and Vondick went to fetch the youngsters who would help with the search of the archives, old retired Abbot Graupulous hung back with Neo the badger Mother.

Graupulous held out the sleeves of his multicolored festival habit. "Just look at this! I feel like a clown in these robes. I never should have let Brae talk me into wearing them, even for a feast day. Of all the days for a Badger Lord to show up at Blackwell, it would have to be the one when I'm dressed up like a traveling show fool!"

"You had no way of knowing such an important visitor would be appearing at our gate this day," Neo consoled him. "If you ask me, Lord Scotus should be glad he came to us on a celebration day he gets to see Blackwell at its very best, with all the food, drink and cheer we're famous for. As for your habit, I think it makes you look rather regal."

"Oh, come now!"

"Well, it is a little ... blinding."

Graupulous made a sour face. "Think I'll run upstairs and put on a proper brown habit of the order ... "

Neo wrapped her massive badger's paw around his shoulder. "Oh, you're just being a temperamental old mouse!"

"I'm a retired Abbot," he said with mock self-importance. "We're allowed to be temperamental. It's a privilege of my station!"

Laughing, the two old friends joined the others at the tables.

Hollnow was acquainting Lord Scotus with the virtues of tater, turnip and beetroot deeper'n'ever pie, a traditional culinary specialty of moles.

"Hurr, zurr, 'ee's not as 'ot as 'ee shudd be, but oi think you'm still loike et."

The badger warrior sampled a forkful from the plate Hollnow had piled high for him, and nodded in satisfaction. Glancing over the tables, he said, "Most creatures in the Northlands go their entire lives without ever seeing this much food in one place."

"Well, this isn't exactly a typical Blackwell meal," Abbess Brae said, some what abashed at this reminder that many creatures did have to survive with far less than the plenty to which the Blackwellers were accustomed. "We do eat well here, even in lean times, but we are ever mindful to share our bounty with less fortunate beasts who otherwise might go hungry."

"A good way to win the hearts and minds of creatures," Dun Scotus observed.

"We act out of charity and decency, not to make alliances," Brother Skara put in quickly. "Things are different here than in the north. We help our fellow creatures because we choose to, and because ... well, it's simply the Blackwell way, that's all." From the corner of his eye Skara saw two small figures making their way toward him from the pond. "Ah! Just the two fine young bellringers I wanted to see! Syril, Serius, I've got a special project I'd like you to help me with."

"Master Vondick told us all about it," Serius blurted out with more enthusiasm than Skara had expected. "We're gonna look through the archives!"

"Well ... yes," Skara smiled uncertainly. "You two seem positively delighted by this, so I guess I picked the right mice for the job."

"An' I'm gonna help 'em!" Grauparus chimed in as he sauntered up behind Syril and Serius. The young otter was clearly forcing himself to seem cheerful about the assignment, for the benefit of the two mice.

Syril had stopped in front of Skara, but his attention was entirely on Dun Scotus. For several moments he just stood and stared at the badger warrior in his red armor. Neo came over to him and playfully ruffled his head fur. "Not polite to stare at our visitors, you young scamp."

"Oh. Er ... sorry." Syril looked up at Dun Scotus, who stood more than twice his own height. "Are you a warrior?" he asked, and then felt his ears start to burn at having asked such an obvious and childish question.

Dun Scotus's face softened. Not an actual smile, but some of the stern grimness melted away.

"Of course," he said, in a voice so natural it made Syril forget his momentary embarrassment.

"I am gonna be a warrior someday," he said before he knew what he was doing, or why. The thought had merely pushed its way to the front of his mind and spilled from his mouth of its own volition.

Neo and the other Abbey leaders stared open mouthed at Syril's wholly unexpected declaration, while his brother Serius plucked a peach tart off the table, stuffed it into his mouth and said, "Me, too," ever mindful of following his sibling's lead.

Skara shook his head. "Syril, I think you've been standing too close to the bells while you've been ringing them."

But Dun Scotus showed no surprise at Syril's statement, and spoke without condescending to the not-quite-adult mouse. "You may wear the habit of a simple Abbey mouse, but a stronger spirit has just voiced itself through you. Follow it, and you will be as great and brave a warrior as you want to be."

"Please, don't encourage him, My Lord," Neo said to her fellow badger. "He's just young and foolish. In a few days he will want to be something else. He's just caught up in the excitement of your arrival. Aren't you, Syril?"

"Uh, er ..." "Perhaps," said Dun Scotus. "But if a beast is destined to become a warrior, then nothing can stand in the way of fate."

"Well, for now these two are our bellringers, as well as our assistant archive-delvers," said Skara. "Their warrior ambitions will just have to wait."

Serius paused in popping another pastry into his mouth. "I wanna read the histories, an' hear all about the wars and battles and villains and ..." His litany was lost in the crumbs of the tart that finally found its way between his jaws.

Skara, ever the peace-loving recorder and historian, merely shook his head. "Where do today's youths get their ideas?"

It was decided that Lord Scotus should stay in the large dormitory room up on the third floor. It was the only available chamber large enough to comfortably accommodate a fully-grown male badger.

The sun had set in fiery summer splendor, and now the gloom of twilight had to be chased from the corridors of Blackwell Abbey by torches, lanterns and candles. As Neo led Dun Scotus up the spiral stone staircase to the uppermost dormitory level, they passed Brother Julius setting alight the night torches that lined the long hallway in recessed sconces. The torch bearing mouse nodded to them respectfully and bade them good night as he hurried off to complete his rounds, bringing the welcome comfort of a warm glow to all of Blackwell's interior.

They halted before a door near the end of the corridor. Neo opened it and ushered Dun Scotus inside. The spacious room was simply appointed with a badger-sized bed, a small table, and a couple of large, deeply-cushioned high back chairs. Two fringed throw rugs lent a cozy air to the chamber by hiding much of the bare floor. Neo set her small lantern down on a shallow wall shelf near the door. The double high windows faced west, and the glorious crimson sky of sunset's afterglow was visible over the western Abbey wall. Enough light from that evening display came through the windows to cast a ruddy hue to the room.

Dun Scotus took in his new surroundings with his traveling warrior's gaze. "Is this your room? It looks tailored to a badger's needs."

Neo shook her head. "There was another Badger Lord who dwelt at Blackwell for some seasons, long before I came here. Calgagus the Axe, Lord of the Western Plains. This was where he dwelt during his time here. It is said that he may have left Blackwell to go in search of your own home Astapailia. By any chance, do you know if he was ever Lord of the Mountain before you?"

Dun Scotus shook his head. "The name is unfamiliar to me. But I do not have every one of my predecessors committed to memory. I am sure he was able to find Astapailia, if it was his fate to rule it."

"Anyway, this room has been maintained thus ever since, in the event that any others of his kind should visit Blackwell. I always thought it was somewhat silly, but now it's almost as if it was being saved for you." Neo shrugged. "Blackwell is a place of spirits. They watch over us, and they may have known you were coming."

"The forces of destiny are not to be underestimated." Dun Scotus crossed the floor to stand at one of the windows. From that vantage he could look out upon the Abbey lawns, the gate house cottage, and the western wall with its main gate. The wall top ramparts came almost up to this level; only be straining could Dun Scotus see the rolling golden swells of the Western Plains beyond, and the misty shadow line of mountains beyond that.

"Quite a view, isn't it?" Neo drew up along side him. "Wait until you see it in the full brilliance of a summer's day, with the green and gold of the plains peeking over the red sand-stone wall at you. I think that's why Calgagus lived up on this floor. Even though he spent many seasons here at Blackwell, it is said he never stopped thinking of himself of Lord of the plains. That was his realm, and he could glimpse it from here, or more fully from the west wall ramparts. In this way, he was able to enjoy both of the places he loved most."

"He was fortunate that there was such a large room available for him up here."
Neo chuckled. "Funny you should say that I thought the same thing when I first moved to Blackwell. But Hollnow soon set me straight on that. Originally, this was two smaller dorms. Hollnow and his crew knocked out the wall to make it a single room that would be comfortably large enough for Calgagus. That's why there are two windows instead of the usual one."

Dun Scotus examined the floor, walls and ceiling between the two windows.
"Seamless work. Your moles are quite skilled."

"No finer mason beasts anywhere," Neo boasted.

"I know some moles up in the Northlands who might care to take up that challenge."
Dun Scotus moved to two small, framed vegetable-dye portraits of female badgers that hung on one wall. "Who are these?"

"I believe one is Calgagus's daughter Vanda, who like me became Blackwell's badger matriarch. The other may be his wife, who passed away when she was quite young I'm not certain. Calgagus painted those himself, you know. Art became a hobby of his during his seasons here, although he was always first and foremost a warrior."

"He was a talented artist. I have dabbled with drawing, although my own interests run more toward architecture."

"Well, I'll leave you to get settled in. Do let us know if you need anything."
Dun Scotus unfastened his sword, shield and axe and laid them on the bed. "Thank you. The hospitality of Blackwell is indeed all that I have heard, and more."

The words and voice were gracious, but still no trace of a smile cracked its way onto Dun Scotus's striped muzzle.

"Good night, My Lord." Neo nodded, and closed the chamber door softly behind her as she exited into the hall. For all of Dun Scotus's grimness, she had to admit to herself that it was good to finally have another badger staying at Blackwell. A male one at that.

In the hour after midnight, Blackwell Abbey slumbered beneath a new summer moon, bright and sharp as a sickle blade in the black, star-pierced mantle of the night sky.

Sister Juliett was quite alone as she tip-pawed up the winding staircase to the top dormitory level, and quietly made her way along the corridor to Dun Scotus's room. As keeper of the Infirmary at Blackwell, she was accustomed to keeping irregular hours since sickness and injury could strike at any hour of the day or night and, since Blackwellers were generally a healthy lot, Sister Juliett often found herself with much free time on her paws, time that she filled by appointing herself to various other sundry tasks. One of these was to help look after the comfort of visitors to the Abbey.

So it was that she now came to be carrying fresh towels and a basin of perfumed water to Dun Scotus's quarters while nearly every other creature of Blackwell lay fast asleep in their bed.

Setting the basin down carefully outside the room, she opened the door a crack and gave thanks that the hinges had been oiled recently. It wouldn't do at all to wake a guest in the middle of the night. Juliett prided herself on her stealth, and being able to come and go without waking even the most skittish rabbit. Retrieving the basin from the floor, she pushed her way into the room.

The only source of light was the lowly guttering wall torch out in the hallway, and it took a moment for Sister Juliett's eyes to adjust to the near-darkness inside the room. Once they had, she gave a surprised gasp and nearly dropped the basin.

Dun Scotus lay upon the bed, propped into a sitting position by pillows against the wall ... and he still wore his full complement of armor, as he had since his arrival at Blackwell. She could tell from the two faint glints in his face that his eyes were open, and he was looking directly at her.

"Oh!" Sister Juliett stammered. "My Lord, I ... I didn't mean to disturb you ... "

"You did not disturb me." The badger's tone was resonant and calm in the darkness, the glint of his eyes unflinching. Juliett felt she was being examined; it was an eerie experience. "You are the healer. Sister Juliett, isn't it?"

"Oh, why, yes." Juliett had only met Dun Scotus very fleetingly at the feast; she wasn't sure they'd even been introduced. Even if he did remember her from the previous afternoon, she was amazed that he could recognize her in the dim illumination from the corridor beyond. "I was just ... uh, bringing you some water and towels, in case you wanted to freshen up in the morning before you came down to breakfast."

"Thank you. That is most thoughtful."

Juliett set the basin upon the small table, folding the towels neatly alongside it. "Do you always sleep in your armor?" she asked, trying to keep her tone light and conversational.

"Who says that I sleep?"

Now Sister Juliett was totally unnerved. She was still a youthful mouse maid, but extremely self-possessed and no-nonsense where her official duties were concerned. Juliett was accustomed to working with uncooperative patients and the occasional nasty injury, and was not easily intimidated by beast or circumstances. But being with Dun Scotus now was unlike anything she'd ever felt before. It was almost like she was conversing with a creature of the spirit world. He was with her here in this room, but he also seemed to dwell elsewhere at the same time.

She edged toward the open door, keeping her face toward the badger warrior.

"Well ... I guess I'll see you in the morning, sir ... uh, Lord. Let us know if there's, er, anything else ... "

"Thank you. I will."

Sister Juliett slid through the opening and closed the door harder than she normally would have so late at night. She stood for a moment gathering her wits back to her, then scurried down the corridor, glad to be away from Blackweller's newest guest.

CHAPTER 3

Gorver and Grauparus were up before sunrise. Two of the Abbey's other younger otters, Cardor and Harden, helped them work the nets in the pond for catches of freshwater shrimp. Gorver had replaced the sword of Septimus in its rightful place in the Great Hall, not wanting to get it wet in the pond. By the time the pale blush of dawn had blossomed into full summer morning, the four of them had hauled in two bulging net-fulls of the tasty crustaceans.

"I think our little pond's getting shrimped out again, Gorver sir," Grauparus said, struggling with his end of one load. "Guess it'll soon be time to make another trip to the River Primley to restock."

"Right you are, Graup laddo! Daresn't let our shrimp pool run low, eh? We'll make a rudder-walloping day trip of it roll out th barrels an' the ol' cart, pack a day's vittles fer all th' otters lads 'n' lasses ... and get Neo to play cart horse. No beast c'n pull that contraption like that great hulking stripe-marm of ours!"

Cardor and Harden were struggling with their burden. "Skipper," Cardor called out, "We're 'avin' trouble liftin' ours."

"Then open the top a scritch an' spill some back inta th' pond. There y'go - good work! Righto, now then, hearties, let's get these li'l wrigglers into th' kitchens. Shrimp 'n' hotroot soup fer lunch t'day, mates! All you can eat!"

Harden sniggered at his companion as they all lugged off for the Abbey. "All we can eat, 'ee says? Not if'n he gets to it first, Cardor matey!"

"I 'eard that!"

The Abbey kitchens were busier than usual for the morning after a feast day. Many Blackwellers would normally skip breakfast altogether following a meal of such proportions, and some would scarcely eat all day. The infants and young ones would never stand for a day without breakfast. This morning, Blackwell had an important guest to think of as well, so there was no question of not opening the kitchens for the morning meal.

Sister Juliett, unable to sleep after her strange encounter with Dun Scotus, had come down to the kitchens to lose herself in labor as she mulled over the experience. Working through the predawn hours, she'd prepared an entire batch of honey bread and had it laid out in pans and ready for the ovens by the time Friar Calgarus joined her.

Now those loaves stood cooling upon racks and table tops, while a second batch was rising in the multi-tiered ovens. The aroma could only be described as heavenly, and as it wafted up through the Great Hall and to the dormitory levels, beasts of all species awoke to greet the day with mouths watering. More than one Blackwell who'd sworn not to eat a thing this morning would be persuaded by their noses to change plans ... which was just fine because there was plenty for every creature at the Abbey.

Unless, of course, Gorver got to them first.

The squad of otters hit the kitchens like an unexpected tidal wave, swinging their heavily-laden shrimp nets this way and that without any regard for life or limb. Friar Calgarus and his helpers had to scatter to get out of the way, while Sister Juliett dove beneath the nearest table.

"Right ho, lads, that's good haulin'! Hey, wot's this? Ah, a reward fer yer hard-workin' Skipper!" In a single smooth motion Gorver flung down his end of the net he and Grauparus were carrying and plucked up one of the cooling loaves. Half of it disappeared in one bite. "Mmmph ... fine bakin'! Think I'll 'ave another ... Ouch!"

Friar Calgarus, recovering from the otter on slaught, had grabbed his favorite ladel and rapped Gorver's paw as the gluttonous creature reached for a second loaf.

Gorver stood rubbing his smacked flipper, a comical look of hurt innocence on his face. "Aw, now why'd y'go an' do that fer, me ol' Friar bucko?"

"Out! Out of my kitchen, you waddling feedbag!" Friar Calgarus stood brandishing his prized utensil. The Friar was a tall, lean whip cord of a mouse, so wiry that some said he merely slipped between gaps in the wall bricks whenever he wanted to leave the Abbey. He was undisputed master of Blackwell's kitchens, and although he probably weighed only a fifth what Gorver did, the otter Skipper was thoroughly cowed by Calgarus's authority here.

Gorver's expression of petulance deepened. "I do not waddle!"

"You have been a plague upon my kitchens every day since I became Friar! Scoffing everything in sight, raiding the stocks, grabbing ingredients while my back's turned ... it's a miracle I've been able to get a single meal prepared with you around! Now, get out!"

"Sorry, matey. Love t oblige, but 'fraid I can't." Gorver's paw shot out for a plate of candied chestnuts. By the time Friar Calgarus's ladel came down, the nut was already in Gorver's mouth. "Y'see, me mateys an' I've got some shrimp stew t'stew up. So clear us some table space, 'cos we got t'get choppin'!"

Friar Calgarus glared at the loaded nets, mortified at the water leaking all over his immaculately clean floor. "Shrimp stew?"

"Shrimp 'n' hotroot soup, to be proper 'bout it. Oh, howdy, Sister Juliett! Wot're you doin' down there? Yes, Friar, seems we didn't 'ave any of our otter soup secialty left over from yesterday, so's we got t'make some more. Got an important guest t' impress, don'tcha know?"

"No leftovers, eh? Wonder why." The Friar heaved a resigned sigh. "Okay, okay. Push those nets off to the side, and as soon as we're done getting breakfast ready, you and your gang can make your soup. But for now, get out! I don't want you scoffing up all my work before it even gets out of this kitchen."

"Nothin' wrongful 'bout scoffin', me dear mouse. A lot t' be said fer it, in fact." Gorver ran his gaze up and down Friar Calgarus. "You should try it yerself. Ain't friars s'posed t' be fat?"

"Two seasons of one's youth spent as a slave will leave its mark on any beast. Maybe if you'd known a little hunger in your own days, you wouldn't be such a glutton now."

"Glutton? Will th' insults never end? Yesterday I was th' guest of honor at me own feast, now I'm just a waddlin', gluttonous feedbag!" Gorver went into a mock swoon, then rounded on his otters. "Right, you 'eard our fry master! Push those nets under th' table an' outta the way whoops! Watch out fer Sister Juliett! an' we'll toddle off fer a bit while the breakfast shift tidies up. There, that's shipshape!" Gorver turned back to Calgarus an snapped an ostentatious salute to the Friar. "There, yer kitchen's back t' you, M'lord Cooker! Call us when th' soup cauldrons are free!"

Even as the quartet of otters trooped off toward the Great Hall, a long, low rumbling came into the kitchen from a tunnel on the opposite end. A large cask appeared from the opening, rolling straight toward the kitchen staff and causing them to scatter once more.

Ularus, the burly hedgehog cellar keeper, appeared on the heels of the barrel, which rolled to a stop in the middle of the floor. Ularus was the master of the drink cellars every bit as much as Friar Calgarus was lord of the kitchens. She peered past the oversized cask, taking in the confusion all about her.

"Quiver my spikes," Ularus said, "I coulda swore I heard that cheeky Skipper of ours, but he don't seem to be about."

"You just missed him and his gang of thieves," Friar Calgarus informed her.

"Thank goodness for that. He'd've quaffed up all my cordial, an' left none fer the Brothers and Sisters."

Sister Juliett stood brushing shrimpnet water from her habit. "Don't you know it, Ularus." She cast an eye toward the barrel. "I say, should you have been rolling it along like that? I thought that would get it all clouded up?"

"Right you are, Julli. This'n here's an empty. T'was leaking a bit, so I drained off the clear portion into flagons fer today's meals. All that's left in here's the dregs. I'll wash her out an' try to patch her up. Failin' that, guess I'll jus' set her out in the cloisters. Might make a good rain barrel, or maybe a planter or somesuch."

"Well, I suppose that means we won't run short of drink this day. What flavor was it?"

"Strawberry. With a bit o' fizz to it."

"Ooo. The little ones will love that. It's their favorite." Juliett glanced about the kitchens. "Fresh warm bread and cold strawberry cordial for all! I think this is going to be a good morning!"

Breakfast was taken that morning on the Abbey lawns. The bright summer sun lit up Blackwell in its full splendor of red masonry and dew-speckled grass, the tiny droplets refracting the sunlight into a million miniature points of rainbow sparkle on the fresh green carpet. Children who'd finished eating ran back and forth on the lawns, heedless of the dawn dampness that wet their footpaws. It was the kind of morning Blackwellers cherished.

The Abbey leaders gathered around a table near the pond. Neo sat alongside Dun Scotus, who'd made a late appearance, while Skara and the Abbess nestled together on a bench across from the two badgers. Even Gorver took a respite from his soup cooking duties to break bread with his companions.

"Glorious Dun Scotus mornin', ain't it?" Makes a beast mighty glad t be alive."

"Yurr, moighty glad indeed,"Hollnow agreed, pouring his third tumbler of the strawberry fizz.

Chewed his bread contemplatively, letting his gaze wander all about him. "Yes, this is a wonderful place you have here. Especially for the youngsters, and the old ones. No such sanctuary as this exists in the Northlands ... although perhaps someday we could build one."

"Wonderful idea!" Gorver muttered through his doughy mouthful. "We can call it Blackwell North ... mebbe open a franchise, exchange emissaries an' all that."

Brae and Skara chuckled at this suggestion, but old Graupulous smiled. "You know, I believe Septimus the Warrior would approve of that idea. He was originally from the Northlands himself, after all. I think he would have built ten Blackwells in his life if he'd been able, throughout the lands, to benefit as many creatures as possible. As it was, Septimus barely lived long enough to see this one finished."

Dun Scotus raised his mug. "A toast then. To Blackwell North!"

"And South, East and West!" Gorver added, hoisting his own cup. "Why stop at one?"

"Multiple Blackwells?" Brae shook her head, laughing. "I'm sorry, but I just can't picture such a thing. Maybe my imagination simply isn't vivid enough, but ... oh, well!" She joined the others in raising her drink in salute. "Here's to as many Blackwells as the good-beasts in all the lands can manage to build and maintain. If that's not the strangest toast I've ever made, then I'm not Abbess!"

Every beast at the table, and a few who stood nearby, laughed and toasted and reveled in the jollity of the moment. All except Dun Scotus, who seemed at ease, but remained solemn and serious.

Brae turned to the badger warrior. "Forgive me if I'm prying, My Lord, but Sister Juliett tells me you slept in your armor last night. That can't have been comfortable!"

Dun Scotus seemed untroubled by the inquiry. "In the north, comfort is a luxury that can get you killed. I realize I am not in the Northlands now, but the habits acquired over many seasons of hardship are not so easily shed."

"Nor is your armor, apparently," Gorver laughed boisterously.

Dun Scotus looked at the otter without smiling. "Just so."

Brother Skara leaned in with a change of subject. "My Lord, I did a little work in the archives last night before going to bed. I've got some of the records you were asking about. I haven't located the Abbey plans yet, but I have a good idea where they might be. It shouldn't take too long to dig them up. If you'd like to come down with me once we've finished breakfast, I can let you have everything you wanted."

"No need for haste," Dun Scotus assured the historian. "First I would like to have a more complete tour of the Abbey than the brief one I was given last night. That should take most of the morning. After that, I can stop down by you to collect the journals and plans. I would prefer to study them in the privacy of my room, where I will be able to concentrate fully. I trust that will give you sufficient time."

"Oh, plenty. They will be waiting, whenever you're ready."

For the second time that morning, the mellow bonging of the twin Maximus and Neltron bells rang out from the bell tower, announcing the official end of mealtime and the start of the day's appointed tasks.

The Abbess gave a chuckle. "I saw Syril and Serius running off toward the tower a moment ago. Those two certainly do immerse themselves in their bellringing duties!"

"Enjoy it while you can, Brae," Neo said, "because once they start helping Skara in the archives and we have to assign some substitute bellringers, I doubt you will hear our two bells ring in such harmony for some time to come."

"Or perhaps never again," Skara said with a smile, "once our young Syril becomes a fearsome warrior and marches off to battle. I can only hope those two apply themselves to our archive search with the same enthusiasm they show toward bellringing!"

That comment met with much merriment among the Blackwellers gathered around the table, and their laughter mingled with the pealing of the twin bells.

Dun Scotus's tour of the Abbey did indeed take until the noon meal. He walked the entire ramparts of the perimeter wall, where he stopped frequently to gaze out over the battlements and scrutinize the lands that led up to Blackwell in all directions. Next he visited Graupulous in his cottage by the main gate, at which point the retired Abbot mouse joined Vondick and young Grauparus as their fellow tour guide for Dun Scotus .

Hollnow conducted the four of them through the underground tunnel system that connected many different parts of the Abbey grounds, then Ularus showed them all the nooks and crannies of her beverage cellars. From there the tour went through the Great Hall, Blackwell's majestic gathering place for indoor feasts and celebrations, and thence up to the Infirmary and all the dormitory levels.

They visited the kitchens on their way back out to the lawns, where the tour ended with a climb to the top of the bell tower. Tall as it was, the tower only reached half as high as the steepled roof peak over the main Abbey. It was in those highest roof spaces that Strongwing held court over the sparrowfolk, or Celtar, of Blackwell. The enormous attic gallery was named Strongbeak Loft, Dun Scotus learned, in honor of a Celtar queen who'd sacrificed herself in battle many seasons before to save Maximus, the warrior mouse who'd rediscovered the long-lost sword of Septimus and defeated the dreaded sea-rat Teivel the Terrible.

"There certainly is a great deal of history attached to your Abbey," Dun Scotus commented on hearing this latest tale as he stared out from the bell tower's open windows.

"That there is," affirmed old Abbot Graupulous. "More than enough to keep any ambitious historian occupied for a lifetime. Brother Skara once tried to count the number of generations that have passed since Blackwell was founded, based on the journals and diaries kept by the various recorders before him. He thinks it's over a hundred, but an exact count is probably impossible."

Dun Scotus nodded. "Can Strongbeak Loft be accessed from inside the Abbey?"

"Not easily," answered Vondick. "There's a hatch door the birds can use to enter the Great Hall, but for the most part the attic spaces are only safely accessible to flying creatures. In an extreme emergency, a squirrel such as myself could climb up from the outside, but it is not an easy feat."

"I would consider that something of an architectural flaw," rumbled Dun Scotus observantly. "Why would your founders design Blackwell so that neither this bell tower nor Strongbeak Loft could be entered from within the safety of the main Abbey?"

"Um ... er ... " No beast at Blackwell was accustomed to having the wisdom of their honored Abbey founders questioned in such an open manner. It left Graupulous and the others literally speechless.

"No matter. Such things can be corrected if need be."

Neo had wanted to be the one to show her fellow badger around Blackwell, but some of the young ones had started acting rambunctious after breakfast, and her strong mother's paw had been required to settle them down. Brae joined Dun Scotus and his escorts for the indoor parts of the tour through the main Abbey, when she wasn't called away to oversee the various routine Abbey matters that always occupied the attentions of Blackwell's Abbots and Abbesses.

The tour now complete, Dun Scotus joined all the Blackwell for lunch out in the orchard. The main course was, of course, Gorver and the otters' shrimp and hotroot soup two cauldrons' worth plus varieties of fresh summer salads, plain and nutted cheeses, more breads from the ovens, and plenty of October ale to wash down the spicy soup. A carousel of several different kinds of fruit pie was wheeled out for those with a sweeter tooth, or who fancied a bite of dessert to follow the main meal. The harmonious tolling, of the twin Maximus and Neltron bells heralded the start of the noontide meal. Since Skara was still getting things in order down in the archives, he'd excused Syril and Serius so that the mouse brothers could engage in their bellringing duties one last time, before immersing themselves in the Abbey records.

The overhanging branches of the orchard's trees provided shady refuge from the hot summer sun, now almost directly overhead. The woodlanders took their meal at leisure; Dun Scotus ate with mechanical efficiency, commenting on the quality of the food and drink, but giving no other sign of pleasure or enjoyment. He finished before most of the others, and strolled over to the edge of the orchard that afforded an idyllic view of the pond.

Gorver, Skara and the Abbess joined the badger warrior. A fish stirred in the distant pond, disturbing the surface with slow ripples that were as lazy as the summer day itself.

"Beautiful spot, isn't it?" Brae said. "I always loved coming here when I was a child, especially on hot days such as this. Just looking at the pond seems to cool a beast off."

Dun Scotus pointed over the pond to the walltop beyond. "If I were an enemy of Blackwell laying siege to this Abbey, and I had large birds in my service, I would prepare bundles of strong poison and have my birds fly high over the wall, out of arrow range, and drop them into your pond, thereby destroying your source of drinking water."

The three Blackwellers stared at him in mortified silence.

Dun Scotus nodded slowly to himself. "That is what I would do, if I were an enemy of Blackwell." Apparently satisfied with this analysis and saying no more, the Badger Lord ambled off toward the gardens, leaving the other three gazing after him.

Gorver was the first to find his tongue. "Cheery fella, that 'un. Must'nt ferget to invite him to our next otter jamboree. He'll be th' life o' the party!"

When lunch was fully over, Gorver and his otters put on a jousting exhibition for Lord Scotus. Many Blackwellers took a break from their afternoon tasks and duties to watch the display.

Forming a wide semi-circle on the lawns near the main gate, the audience "ooed" and "ahhd" and applauded as Graupuss put his juniors through their paces with drills that were part javelin and quarter staff duels and part acrobatic maneuvers. Dun Scotus watched the exercises with rapt intensity. He seemed thoroughly engrossed by the militaristic exhibition. It was the closest he'd come to having an out-and-out good time that any of the Blackwellers had seen so far.

Vondick and his squirrel companion Woody walked over to Graupuss when the proceedings were concluded. "Trying to make us look bad, you old ruddertail?" he asked his otter friend with mock anger. "Grabbing all the glory for yourselves ... I'll bet we squirrels of the Forest Patrol could put on an archery display that would hold Lord Dun Scotus's attention just as well."

"Betcher could too, ol' chum." Graupuss was sweaty and breathing hard from his exertions. "But we thought of it first. Now, I'm off fer a splash an' a swim in th' pond. Awful hot in this sun, an' I daresn't offend, eh?" With that, he shot off toward the inviting coolness of the pond and dove in, Grauparus and most of the other otters hot on his heels. The two squirrels stood watching them cavort for a bit, showing off their swimming skills for anybeast who cared to watch, or for no-beast at all.

"Woody," Terious said.

The other squirrel straightened to attention at the formal tone of command in Vondick's voice. They were old friends and both around the same age, but when Terious asserted his authority as head of the Primley Patrol, Woody was quick to fall in line. "Yes, sir?"

"Prepare some targets by the gardens, and password among the others of the Patrol. After dinner tonight, we'll put on a little show of our own."

"Yessir!"

CHAPTER 4

As soon as they were finished ringing the bells for the end of lunch, Syril and Serius rushed down from the bell tower to join Brother Skara in the archives.

For most of its history, Blackwell's historians and recorders had lived in the small cottage by the main gate, and it was in that gate house that the Abbey records had been kept. After the war with Teivel's horde, however, old Abbot Sandow had ordered that the little hut be expanded into a rambling cottage for Blackwell's new Warrior, Maximus, and his wife Sinead. That meant that a new home had to be found for all the books, scrolls, tablets, parchments, maps, drawings and other assorted odds and ends that comprised the Abbey archives.

For several generations they had been deposited willy-nilly in any unused chambers that could be found, but the solution to this dilemma had lain quite literally under every-beast's nose all along. During an earlier siege by a conquering raven, the moles had devised a network of tunnels under the Abbey's grounds to confound the raven warlord, so that the Blackwellers might come and go as they pleased without danger of attack from their winged foe. Once the invading birds had been vanquished and peace restored to the Abbey, the mole crews had improved upon the hastily-built tunnels, properly lining them to make them a permanent part of Blackwell.

Since so much work had already gone into the tunnel system, it was little extra effort for the moles of a later generation to dig out and line an additional dead end, spacious enough to hold the entire contents of the archives, plus room for future generations to add to it. This rock-lined chamber now served as the official Blackwell library.

Unfortunately, the historical records had never been kept in a particularly orderly manner, even when they'd been stored up in the gatehouse. When Skara inherited the post of official recorder from his predecessor Brother Rampor, he also inherited quite a disorderly mess to oversee. Most of Blackwell's historians had contented themselves with keeping their own journals, and simply let lie all the tangled chaos of what had come before, delving into the past only when a particular bit of historical fact needed to be produced and then it usually took a heroic effort to find it. Skara had sworn to change all that. He was going to make his lifelong work the organizing of the archives into some system that did not hinge upon guesswork, intuition or magic. His goal was to build a library that any Blackweller could use with ease, to access any period of Abbey history without having to dig through disordered masses of scrolls and journals.

The shifting of the archives from the gate house to assorted rooms and then to this tunnel hadn't helped matters any. Skara had been Abbey recorder for several seasons now, yet still he resided over a mayhem of scribblings.

His duties as Blackwell's teacher had kept him from spending as much time on his pet project as he would have liked, and then of course there were his own journals and diaries that he had to keep current; it wouldn't do at all for future generations to have no records of these times. Hollnow had been about to help build a system of racks and partitions that would help bring order to the situation, but then Lord Scotus had arrived and that project had once been placed on the backburner. Skara sighed and glanced about him. Spacious as they were, the archives were now crowded with the extra table and chairs that had been brought down for Syril, Serius and Grauparus. When Dun Scotus had appeared a short time ago for the items he'd requested, the badger had to stand at the tunnel entrance while they were passed out to him.

Getting rid of those few pieces had barely made a dent in the vast walls and piles of records. Fortunately, the work Skara had done that morning and the previous night had paid off; he'd been able to uncover some of the very earliest historical records, a few going all the way back to the days of Septimus the Warrior and the Abbess Grethin, when the Abbey had still been under construction. It was there that their search for clues about Dun Scotus's prophecy would begin.

Skara held up one bound volume with extreme reverence. "This is the oldest journal I could find," he told the two young mice Grauparus had yet to join them from his midday swim in the pond.

"It is written in the ancient script of Stoneridge, of which I understand a little, and seems to have been put down by the Abbess Grethin herself. The paper is quite fragile with age, so I'll keep this one for myself." He set the book down at his place on the table, then turned to a collection of scrolls.

"These parchments date from around the same time, I think, or a little later. They are also quite delicate, so be careful how you unroll them. They are in normal script, so you should have no trouble reading them. Grauparus can help you with them, if he ever finishes cavorting in the pond and deigns to join us. That one has a scholarly future ahead of him here at the Abbey, but sometimes I think there's too much otter in him for his own good!"

Syril and Serius laughed. Grauparus, a couple of seasons older than Syril, was a good friend of theirs. They knew he was probably Skara's best student ... and they also knew what the recorder mouse meant by Grauparus having too much otter in him. Sometimes, when the Abbey pond or a jousting companion had beckoned, Grauparus had been known to forget all about his schooling and skip class altogether.

"And if any beast has to sneeze, please ... turn your head away from what you're reading!"

Skara had very good reason to mention this last bit. When the archive tunnel had first been dug and lined generations ago, there was concern over excessive dampness that might creep through the stones and harm the cloth, paper and bark of the records. Hollnow had solved that problem by coating floor, walls and ceiling with a special chalky powder that kept the chamber quite dry. The downside to this remedy was that the fine dust often agitated the nose if it was inhaled for any length of time. The ancient records had been dusty enough of their own accord; the drying powder only made sneezing all the more likely and, one simply did not sneeze on documents penned by Blackwell's most revered figures.

The young brothers had come prepared. Syril and Serius each withdrew a clean white kerchief from their habits and proudly displayed them for Skara to see. "Fresh from the laundry basket," Syril proclaimed.

"'though I don't think they will stay that way for long," Serius added, his whiskers already starting to twitch from the dust.

"Well, keep them close at paw, then." Skara moved one of the table lanterns closer to him and tilted it so that its light shone more directly upon the pages of the ancient journal before him. Adjusting the glasses perched upon the end of his snout, he leaned down toward the open book.

"We've got a lot of work ahead of us, my friends, so let's get reading!"

Ularus was rolling her empty barrel around the Abbey grounds, looking for a good spot for it. Scrubbed clean of its sticky strawberry juice residue, the over sized cask was now ready to be used as a rain collector. It was just a matter of finding the right place for it …

A shadow passing over her made the hedgehog cellar keeper stop and look up. Wincing through the bright afternoon sky glare, Ularus could make out the shape of a large bird of prey, winging its way north over the Abbey.

Ularus fought her first impulse to run for cover. Before she'd settled at Blackwell, she'd spent her early childhood living in the wilds of southern Primley, and woodland creatures had to develop a healthy respect for predators if they wanted to reach old age. But no hunter would dare to attack within the sanctuary of Blackwell, in case it might someday require refuge or healing from the Abbey for itself. Ularus shook off her case of nerves and was about to resume rolling her barrel, when something made her glance skyward again.

The bird dipped lower as it neared the north wall. For a moment it seemed about to alight upon the battlements, but it cleared the walltop and then was gone.

Ularus scrunched up her eyes, rubbing at them with both paws. She could have sworn ... No, it must have been the summer sun, making her see things that weren't there. No wild bird would be wearing armor. It was impossible. Ularus put her head down and went back to pushing the barrel across the lawns.

Meanwhile, across the Abbey grounds, Grauparus was hauling himself out of the pond and shaking the water from his fur in preparation for joining Brother Skara, Syril and Serius down in the archives. Bidding his fellow otters farewell until dinnertime, Grauparus sauntered toward the main Abbey, but was stopped by a somewhat unusual sight. Three of the Abbey youngsters Ularus's nephew Rufus, along with Sass the dormouse and Gastron the mole stood in the middle of the lawns, necks craned as they gazed to the heavens with paws to brows. Their wooden swords, a requirement for playing the favorite game of "Septimus the Warrior," hung limply at their sides, and that was the strange thing. Blackwell's children were an energetic lot, and Rufus more so than most, so it was out of the ordinary to see them so still. Grauparus was popular with the Abbey children, and paused to kneel alongside the rapt trio to investigate. He addressed them in the more traditional otter jargon that he knew they found entertaining. "Ahoy there, me liddle buckos! Wot're we lookin' at?"

Rufus, the unspoken leader of any gang he happened to be in, pointed straight up. "There's a big bird up there!"

"Oh?" Grauparus followed their gazes, screwing up his eyes against the sky's brightness. Sure enough, there was a bird circling high over the Abbey and, not just any bird. It was a big one, surely a bird of prey, and quite possibly dangerous, especially to creatures as small as his current companions.

The young otter glanced about the grounds. Ularus was off in the distance, working with a barrel, and beyond that, by the gardens, Vondick and Woody were busy setting up a line of archery targets near the gardens. Ularus was reassured that there were other able beasts nearby he could call on for help in case the bird attacked, and decided to stay with the children for a while, to see what this unknown visitor to their air space would bring.

Ularus, Grauparus and the children were not the only ones to notice the circling raptor. As the bird's shadow chased and danced across the Abbey grounds, Vondick and Woody glanced up to see it, as did Graupuss and several of the other otters still lounging in or by the pond.

Soon a small crowd was gathered on the lawn, necks thrown back and paws to their eyes as they strained against the summer brightness to get a better view of the mysterious winged stranger. Even Brae and Graupulous came out to join the spectators.

"What do you make of it, Vondick?" the Abbess asked. The squirrels had the sharpest vision of all the assembled beasts.

"I'm not sure. I thought at first it might be a kite, but it's more like a brown falcon, though it's hard to be certain with the sun's glare."

"Has it threaten or tried to attack any beast?" Graupulous asked with concern.

"No, it's just been circling, sometimes low, sometimes high like it is now," Terious replied.

"Reckon there's more'n one?" Grauparus supposed. "That bird stayin' over us could just be a diversion."

"A diversion for what?" asked Brae.

Grauparus shrugged. "Dunno. Just wondrin' aloud, is all."

"Haven't seen signs of any others," said Terious. "It seems to be alone."

They all stood in silence for a while, studying the newcomer. As they watched it swooped lower, although it was still well above the Abbey roof peaks.

Keen-eyed Vondick broke the silence. "You know, I could swear that bird's wearing something over its breast. A jerkin, or a tunic ... "

"Yes, I thought I noticed that myself," echoed Brae. "But I thought I was seeing things." Ularus put in, "Thought it was armor, myself, when I first saw it flying low over the north wall."

"Maybe we should try to contact it," Brae suggested. "I wonder if the Celtar know anything about this? I haven't seen Strongwing since breakfast. Perhaps we could get one of our sparrows to fly up and ask it what it wants."

There was a special signal the Blackwellers could sound on the Maximus and Neltron bells that would summon the sparrows down from Strongbeak Loft in time of need. "I don't know if we should trouble our Celtar friends about this just yet,"Graupulous said. "If it wants anything of us, it'll fly down here to let us know."

"Unless it's scared,"Terious speculated. "There is quite a crowd of us here, and we Blackwellers do have a reputation for defending ourselves well against all threats."

"It has been many, many seasons since we've had to fight off an enemy," old Graupulous countered. "Not even in my lifetime has the sword of Septimus been used in battle."

"Well, it wants something," Ularus said. "Wouldn't be hangin' about like that if'n it didn't."

"Maybe it's injured," Brae ventured.

"A hurt creature t'wouldn't be soaring about all over the sky," Ularus objected.

"What if it is hurt in the leg?" Woody suggested. "Then it could fly all it wanted but, it wouldn't land ... just like it's doing now."

"Hey, that's good thinkin'!" Graupuss clapped the squirrel on the back.

"Woody may be right." Brae turned to the hedgehog cellarkeeper. "Ularus, would you please run down to the archives and tell Skara that he will have to spare Syril and Serius for a few minutes? I want to signal the Celtar, and they're the only ones skilled enough on the bells to ring the proper sequence."

"On my way,"Ularus said with her usual gruffness, and made for the Abbey. Going in, she passed Lord Scotus, who was just walking out onto the lawns. The badger warrior was alone, and stopped to look at all the Blackwellers who were gazing skyward. "Am I missing something interesting?" he rumbled in his deep voice.

"Just a falcon in armor,"Vondick said half-jokingly.

Dun Scotus followed their gazes until he sighted the bird for himself. "Ah, that would be Crsypin. Excuse me a moment."

Before his words had even registered on the Blackwellers, Dun Scotus was striding across the lawn toward the west wall. He rapidly ascended the wall stairs up to the ramparts, and took up a position on the highest point above the main gate.

Unsheathing his mighty sword, he held it straight out over his head and twirled it in slow circles, once, twice, three times. The sun glinting off the blade's edges and his armor must have been visible halfway across the Western Plains.

Dun Scotus sheathed his weapon and stood still as stone, gaze fixed upon the aerial visitor, waiting. He did not have to wait for long.

The giant bird dropped toward him like a rock. The watching Blackwellers gasped in alarm. The winged hunter's power dive seemed designed to crash into the badger and hurl him from the heights of the wall top. But at the last moment it executed an impressive breaking maneuver and alighted smoothly upon the crenellated stone battlements alongside Dun Scotus.

"Well, I'll be ... " muttered Graupulous, with similar pronouncements from several of the others.

"Never seen anything fly like that before," Vondick remarked.

The badger and the falcon which was indeed wearing a heavy sleeveless breast tunic, unheard of for a bird - appeared to have gone into a rapidfire conference with each other.

"It would seem they are acquainted," Brae said, dryly stating the obvious.

Moments later, the falcon took off once more, winging its way north until it was lost to view. Dun Scotus descended the wall steps to rejoin the Blackwellers. To their amazement, he walked right past them and seemed about to re enter the Abbey without so much as a word of explanation.

"Uh ... My Lord," Brae called after him. "Could you please enlighten us as to what all that was about?"

Dun Scotus stopped and turned back toward the Abbess. "That was Crsypin, a Captain of my forces. He bore reports of the fighting to the north. It has gone well this day."

"Fighting?" Graupulous asked with unease.

Dun Scotus nodded. "A band of crows and ravens who fancied themselves warlords and conquerers were causing no small amount of misery. My fighters engaged them on the northern fringes of Primley, several day's march from here. Those villains will trouble good beasts no more."

"You have fighters, here in Primley?" Brae inquired of Dun Scotus, most surprised by this revelation.

"Far to the north, quite some distance from Blackwell. Some of my more loyal follow-ers traveled south with me for part of the journey, although the bulk of my forces remain in the true Northlands to keep order there as best they can in my absence."

"Well, how many are now near Primley? Should we expect to see them here at Black-well?"

"They may make their way here, in time," replied Dun Scotus. "Crsypin and his breth-ren will keep me apprised of their movements. I cannot give an exact number since they may divide along different routes according to any opposition they meet, and some may turn back north.

But I should be able to give you a day or two's notice if they come on toward Black-well, so that you can make ready to receive them."

This had been Brae's main concern. "We'd appreciate that, My Lord. Tired and hungry warriors should have a proper welcome, and that takes time. Also, if there are inju-ries among any of your creatures, Sister Juliett can prepare the Infirmary for them."

Dun Scotus nodded his appreciation. "Also, a storm is blowing in from the east. A very strong one. It should arrive before sundown."

Several of the Blackwellers looked up at the cloudless expanse of azure sky. There was neither sight nor scent of any trace hint on the hot summer afternoon air that bad weather might be bearing down on them.

Graupulous's nose wrinkled and his whiskers twitched as the gave the windless air a good long sniff. "Are you sure, My Lord?" he asked. "I can't detect any signs of a change in the weather, and I'm usually pretty good about such things."

"That he is," Brae affirmed of her elderly predecessor. "So am I and I can't feel a thing that says a storm is coming. Not a cloud in the sky, either."

The Badger Lord was impassive. "Crsypin is never wrong about such matters. A storm is coming. I have given you warning. What you do with that information is up to you." Dun Scotus turned and went inside, leaving the Blackwellers wondering at both his attitude and his forecast.

Moments later, Ularus emerged from the main Abbey building, bustling before her the two bellringers she'd been sent to fetch. Syril and Serius looked positively ghostly, coated as they were by the chalky drying powder of the archives. Children and adults alike had to laugh at the sight.

"Sorry to have pulled you away from your work with Brother Skara," Brae said, surpressing her chuckles, "but we won't be needing your bellringing talents after all. We were able to solve this mystery without calling on the Celtar. You two can get back to what you were doing since I can see, ah, er, um, that you were quite immersed in it." Unable to contain herself any longer, Brae began to giggle like a little schoolmouse.

Ularus was not so amused. "You mean I ran all the way down to those musty old archives fer naught? Why, what happened? What was with that bird?"

"Turned out it was one of Lord Scotus's captains," Vondick explained, and told Ularus about how the badger had called Crsypin down to get the falcon's reports on fighting to the north of Primley, and the approaching storm. The hedgehog was as incredulous as any beast about the last part.

"Storm? Not if'n you ask me. Can't feel it in my spikes, an' I allers do. That featherbag must be mistaken."

"Well, we'll know soon," said Brae. "Lord Scotus told us it would come before sundown, and that's only a few hours away." She looked down at Syril and Serius. "If we do get a storm, it might be good for you two. You could stand out in the rain to wash away all that dust. Skara too, if I know him!"

The Blackwellers began laughing anew at the two white-dusted, forlorn-looking mouse brothers. Syril grinned, then joined in on the mirth. Serius merely sneezed.

CHAPTER 5

For the next two hours, the deceptive calm of a sunny summer afternoon held sway. When the storm begins, it crept up secretly and low to the ground like a hunter stalking its prey. But it did not catch the good creatures of Blackwell completely off guard.

Neo was walking a group of the Abbey children along the ramparts around the wall tops, giving them some exercise and fresh air, as well as a chance to expend some of their youthful energy that might otherwise run her ragged.

As their line snaked its way over the eastern wall, Neo happened to glance out over the fastness of Primley Woods. But it was what she saw on the distant horizon above the treetops that made her stop dead in her tracks, and her young charges with her.

"By all my seasons!" she exclaimed, staring at the ominous black cloud banks that were rearing up into the sky and rolling toward Blackwell. The afternoon around her was still bright and sunny, and no beast down on the Abbey grounds could possibly have guessed that something so evil was visible from up here.

"That old falcon of Dun Scotus's was right! Storm's on its way, and it looks like a monster!"

Several of the young beasts cowered at the mention of a monster storm, but the irrepressible Rufus was excited by this news. The young hedgehog jumped so he could latch his paws onto the stone work of the battlements and peer up and out over the wall top.

"Wow!" he said with unbridled enthusiasm. "It looks like the end of the world!"

"Down from there, you spiny troublemaker!" Neo turned to address the whole group. "Listen, we're the first ones to see this, and we've got to let the rest of the Abbey know. By the way, it's moving that storm will be here in less than an hour. We'll go down the east wall steps over there, carefully so that no beast falls. When we're down, I want each of you to go find an adult, and tell them a bad storm's coming. Can we all do this?"

The Blackwell children all nodded obediently. When Neo took charge like this, there was nothing to be afraid of, and no thought of being disobedient. Even Rufus fell sharply in to step as she herded them down the tall flight of stone stairs to the lawn below.

She escorted them as far as the door into the Great Hall, except for Sass the dormouse who saw his father working in the orchard and raced off to him. The rest Neo ushered into the Abbey building, where she instructed them to scatter and raise the alarm about the approaching storm. Hopefully most would obey, although they were children after all. The important thing had been getting them safely indoors before the tempest arrived.

If they were less than diligent about performing the task assigned them, well, Neo could raise the alarm perfectly well on her own. All she'd have to do was find Brae, or Graupulous, or Graupuss or Vondick, or any of the Abbey leaders. She paused before the threshold. She'd been about to go inside when the bell tower caught her eye. Neo contemplated it for a few moments, then shrugged to herself and started toward the tall structure.

"How hard can it be?" she mused aloud.

Bong!

All over the Abbey, creatures who had not been alerted by the children stopped in the middle of what they were doing and looked up at the sound of the Maximus bell. Even old Graupulous stirred from his afternoon nap, and poked his head out his gate house cottage door. It was widely known that no temporary bell-ringers had been assigned to replace Syril and Serius. Furthermore, it was not an hour at which the bells should have been tolling. Since the bells were traditionally used to sound warnings as well as celebrate joyous occasions, every Blackweller was trained from infancy to heed their melodious calling, day or night.

A few of the adults did know what was going on, thanks to the young messengers Neo had dispatched. But most were mystified, and went to look out a window or go outside to find out who was ringing the bells, and why.

Boom! Bong!

The Neltron bell now joined its voice to its companion.

 stood up in the belfrey, one bell rope grasped in each massive paw. She knew the ringing sequence for a storm alarm and she was pretty sure she could toll it out herself, once she got things going.

But it turned out to be trickier than she'd imagined. Each bell had its own feel as it swung upon its axle, and the delay between pulling on the rope and actually producing a sound made it difficult to co-ordinate the twin bells.

Her size and strength gave her an advantage. No other beast at Blackwell could have rung both bells at once by itself. Since they were both under her control, Neo was soon able to get into the rhythm of pulling and pealing, and she began to toll out the warning that would alert the Abbey that a storm was on the way.

Old Graupulous was waiting for Neo outside the bell tower when she came down. He greeted her with a smile of amusement.

"A war alarm, Neo? I didn't know Blackwell was under attack."

The badger's face fell. "Oh dear, did I really? I could have sworn I was ringing out a storm warning."

Graupulous shook his head. "You had the half-tones reversed during the second part of the sequence. Still, though that was pretty impressive for such an impromptu performance. Do we get an encore?"

"That depends upon the audience reviews." Neo was looking past him toward the Abbey. A group headed by Abbess Brae was hastening their way. "I hope I haven't caused too much trouble by sounding the wrong alarm."

Graupulous regarded the on coming Abbey dwellers. "They don't look armed for war to me."

Brae came right up to them. "Neo, was that you on the bells?"

"Under them, actually," Neo hastily explained. "There's a storm on the way, I saw it from the wall top, and I wanted to sound the alarm, and I thought I could do it myself, only now Graupulous tells me the sequence wasn't right, and I was off a bit, and it ended up sounding like a war alarm, and "........

Brae held up both her paws. "Neo, please, before you wind yourself! We know it was a storm warning, the young ones told us. You're to be commended. Now we'll have plenty of time to prepare, thanks to you!"

Vondick, standing behind the Abbess, nodded. "Yes, I'd say we've found our new bellringer."

"With a little more practice," Graupulous playfully chided.

"Come on, every beast!" Brae clapped her paws sharply. "We've got work to do, before the wind blows up and the rain starts to fall." She began issuing instructions to her fellow Blackwellers to make preparations. Even now the first clouds were visible over the east wall, and a cool breeze had begun to stir the warm afternoon air.

Leaving the ground work to others, Neo made for the Abbey. There were the young ones to look after and keep out of their parents' way. If this storm turned out half as bad as it had looked from the wall top, there would surely be many frightened infants who would need her comforting paw in the night to come.

Vondick and his squirrels never did get to display their archery skills after that evening's meal.

By the time dinner rolled around, a heavy, wind-driven rain was pelting the Abbey and its grounds, saturating the gardens, orchard and lawns and making it unsafe to venture outdoors. The frequent flashes of lightning were so bright that they could be seen even down in the Great Hall, and the booming crashes of thunder were enough to set pots and pans clattering in the kitchen. Outside on the eastern lawn, Vondick's archery targets stood unused and abandoned, getting drenched by the down pour

The storm had also brought with it a drastic drop in temperature. The hot summer afternoon quickly became a distant memory as an almost autumnal chill blew in on the winds. Many Blackwellers hastened to wrap extra cloaks or shawls around themselves and the youngsters, while some traded their light summer garb altogether for the heavier clothing of colder seasons.

The dinner table benches in the Great Hall were packed that night. This grand gathering space of Blackwell was easily large enough to seat all hundred and some-odd creatures who currently called the Abbey home, with plenty of room to spare. Extra torches were lit around the walls and sandstone columns to help chase away the dispiriting gloom of the early, storm-induced twilight.

Abbess Brae led the assemblage in an offering of thanks for Blackwell's plenty, and then every beast promptly tucked in. The main course was a thick vegetable stew with dumplings, and side salads of radish, leek or beet root, according to each creature's taste. There were also loaves of spice bread and acorn muffins with blackcurrant jam and - at the insistance of Rufus and his young followers - a selection of puddings for dessert, topped by Friar Calgarus's delectable blend of honey-sweetened whipped cream. Ularus and Gorver made sure there was plenty of Octoble ale and elderberry wine for all, with clear cool water and the leftover strawberry cordial for the young ones.

When dinner was winding down and every beast had its fill (except for Gorver, who was filling his plate for the third time), Vondick said to Dun Scotus, "Nights like this are made for the telling of stories. Share some tales or songs with us, My Lord. You must have many, after all your travels and adventures."

Others nearby leaned forward, ears pricked up, eager to hear what the badger warrior would come up with.

Dun Scotus cast his gaze toward Neo, who'd spent the better part of dinner time making rounds throughout the Great Hall, comforting all the younger children who were scared of the storm. Several times, lightning had flashed so brightly and thunder had exploded so loudly that the peak of Blackwell most surely had been struck. Even now, a cluster of young ones skirted Neo around her bench, afraid to stray too far from the badger Mother of Blackwell.

"Alas, those are rough tales to tell, and I would not speak of such things with females and children about. This weather has caused enough fright, and I would not add to that mood with tales of dread and misery that would be hard to take even in the full light of day."

Dun Scotus turned to Brother Skara, who'd reluctantly taken off from his archival search to join his fellow Abbey dwellers for dinner. "As guest here, I would request that we look instead to a tale of Blackwell itself. I was reading in my room this after- noon of the climb your hero Maximus made up to the roof spaces in his quest for the lost sword of Septimus. I would like to hear more of that adventure, if you can embellish it further."

Several gazes at the table lifted to the ceiling high overhead. This was a tale well- known to nearly every Blackweller.

Skara cleared his throat. "Erhem. Ah, well, since I'm the historian here and probably better acquainted with that episode of our history than anybeast here, I suppose I'll start. Oh, but it makes my head dizzy just thinking of that climb! How Maximus did it I'll never know."

"He was a warrior," Dun Scotus said simply. "In time of need, a warrior knows no fear."

"Perhaps. But Maximus was a warrior without a weapon, and the horde of Teivel the Terrible had Blackwell under siege. Clues hidden all around the Abbey told Maximus that Septimus's sword could be found on the weathervane, up on the highest roof peak. This was before the sparrows had become our allies, and the Celtar leader was quite mad and very dangerous. When it was discovered that the sword was no longer on the weathervane and that the Celtar had most likely stolen it, Maximus was left no choice but to climb up to their court under the high roof spaces to con- front them and try to get it back."

Skara squinted toward the high part of the wall above the gallery, then pointed. "If your eye sight is very keen - as mine was in my youth, but alas, is no more - you might be able to make out the opening in the stone work, which is where Maximus emerged from the attic over the dormitories.

That was as high as he could get from the upper dorm level, and the drop from there to this floor would kill any beast. Yet, as you can see - uh, can you see, My Lord? ah, good - as you can see, that's only about halfway to the ceiling of the Great Hall. From there Maximus had to climb along stone ledges, up along one of the roof arches to the highest window casement, and from there to a trap door into the roof spaces under the highest peak." Skara shuddered. "That surely must have been as great a challenge for young Maximus as it was to actually face Teivel the Terrible himself in battle!"

"And at the end of his climb, he still had to face the hostile Celtar?"

"Yes," Skara nodded. "Those must have been harrowing times, and if the spirit of Septimus had not been strong within Maximus and helped guide and protect him, Blackwell might have been lost. But Maximus made a good friend in King Bull Celtar's niece Strongbeak, who became queen after her uncle was killed. Thanks to her, the Celtar became true and faithful allies to Maximus and his son Julien during their time as Abbey Champions."

"Very true." The Abbess glanced up at the ceiling. "And that friendship was rekindled in my own youth by Strongwing, who now rules the Celtar of Strongbeak Loft. Our feathered friends can't be enjoying this storm very much. I do hope they're all right up there. A couple of those lightning strikes sounded like they must have hit the roof."

"They heard Neo's storm bells," Vondick assured her. "They chose to ride out the storm up in Strongbeak Loft. I'm sure they will be fine. Blackwell has weathered many storms before this."

"It would seem to me," Dun Scotus commented in his casual rumble, "that there should be some easy way to access the roof spaces from inside the Abbey. I would call that a rather serious design flaw by those who planned Blackwell."

"So you said this morning in the bell tower," Vondick responded. Others, who had not heard of the Badger Lord's earlier criticism of their Abbey's hallowed founders, bristled a bit at this off-the-paw remark from the grim warrior. On the other paw, Dun Scotus had a very good point.

"Well, nothing to be done about it now,"Brae said with forced cheerfulness. "We wood landers live in the lower parts of Blackwell, and we trust to the Celtar to look after the roof spaces. That arrangement has served us well for many seasons now."

"Yes, but what if you had to visit the Celtar in their Loft?" Dun Scotus pressed. "Is some beast going to make the same dangerous climb that Maximus made all those seasons ago? When the raven General Gerome tried to conquer Blackwell, he took over the roof spaces and could attack you from there at will, but there was no way for you to strike back at him. Would it not have been better if you could have taken the battle to him?"

"My, you have been studying our histories," Skara said, impressive!

"What would you have us do?" Brae said rather more testily than she'd intended, fixing Dun Scotus with a searching and somewhat critical gaze of expectation. She did not seriously expect an answer.

The Badger Lord reached into a space in his breast armor and withdrew a sheet of paper. "Here is one possible solution ... an idea I was toying with this afternoon. I worked up a few rough sketches. We could build a stair case from the Great Hall to Strongbeak Loft."

Brae took the sheet from Dun Scotus and studied it. Immediately her fellow Black-wellers sidled over to her on the bench or came around to stand behind her, curious to view the sketch over her shoulder. Proper dinner manners were suspended for the moment as creatures crowded their Abbess to see this for themselves.

The drawing that Dun Scotus had tossed out as little more than a doodle proved instead to be a highly detailed architectural rendering, complete with notes, measurements, and scale references. It depicted, unmistakably, an enclosed, winding staircase rising from the floor of the Great Hall to the highest roof spaces in a single unbroken spiral of steps.

Brae exhaled in disbelief. "Is such a thing possible?"

"One way to find out," said old Abbot Graupulous, scanning the faces around the tables until he spotted the one he sought. "Hullo, Hollnow! Come over here, please. We have a matter that requires your expertise."

The squat digger excused himself from his place at table with his customary mole politeness and waddled across to where his Abbess sat. "Ho hurr, 'ow can oi be o''elp, gennel beasts?"

"Lord Scotus has proposed a most impressive undertaking." Brae passed the sketch to Hollnow. "You're our expert at such things. Tell us what you think of this."

Hollnow took a gander at the plans. After a moment, once he realized what he was looking at, his nearly-invisible button eyes widened to twice their normal size ... which was quite comical to behold.

"Huuurrzzuurwuuu ... " Hollnow glanced up from the sketch toward the end of Great Hall where the plans placed the stairs, then back down at the paper. He repeated this motion several times. "Boi okey, oi'm a-seein' et but oioi doant berlieve et. Starway t'eaven, hurr hurr."

"Do you think it can be built?" Brae asked.

"Burr, doant see no reasern whoi not. 'ee archertekshual theory's sound enuff. But oi wuddn't want t'be th' beast that builds it. Uz molers doant be moighty fond o' gurt 'oights, no zurr."

"The stairs would be enclosed by their own well wall and anchored to the main wall of the Great Hall," Dun Scotus said, "so there wouldn't be much danger of worker-beasts fallings during construction."

Brae was uncertain. "Such a project would require much time and great effort from many Blackwellers. Are you sure it's really necessary, My Lord?"

"You are the ones who have lived here for generations without it. Only you can say. But you have engaged me to help you with matters of defense, and from that standpoint, I would strongly urge that the stairs be built."

Dun Scotus repositioned himself so he could point at the plans in Hollnow's claws. "You will notice the design calls for a door at the top that can be locked from either side. If your roof spaces should ever again fall to enemy war birds, you could lock them out from below and deny them access to the Abbey proper. By the same token, if an enemy horde were ever to breach the Abbey walls, your children and old ones could take refuge with the Celtar in Strongbeak Loft while the fighting goes on below. There is room to store enough provisions up there to last out a siege of a season or more."

Old Graupulous shook his head. "I don't know. Speaking as one of the 'old ones,' I for one would not want to be stuck up there with no way down if the lower Abbey were to fall to an enemy. Seems to me it would just be a matter of time before they'd break through and have us at their mercy."

"The positioning of the door at the top of the stair case would make it very awkward to employ a battering ram or any other tools of force to open it," Dun Scotus said. "If food supplies ran low during a prolonged siege, the Celtar could forage outside the Abbey for re-stocks. You must learn to use your birds to their full potential; they are a most important resource. Rain barrels under the eaves would keep water in supply in all but the driest seasons.   In battle, it is very important to have options. These stairs would provide Blackwell with options it does not have now."

Brae was still doubtful. "I have great friendship with the Celtar, and I more than any beast would welcome a way to visit them in Strongbeak Loft. I just can't help wondering whether these stairs would be worth all the work of building them."

"I can only give you the benefit of my warrior's counsel," Dun Scotus said to the Abbey leaders around him. "The final decision in such matters must of course be yours."

"In this case," said Brae, "not just ours alone. The Celtar must be consulted as well. It wouldn't do at all for us to just pop out of their court floor one day and say, 'Surprise!' They must also approve of these stairs before we can even consider building them."

Another flash of lightning lit up the Great Hall through the high stained glass windows. The crack of thunder that came with it was ear-splitting, the sound of the very air being rent as under followed by a boom that made bones vibrate in their flesh. Several of the children squealed in fright and huddled closer around Neo.

Gorver looked up from his fourth plateful without missing a beat in his chewing. "Another direct him, by me rudder," he opined around a mouthful of damson and apple pudding.

Brae shook her head. "Those poor sparrows. I don't envy them on a night like this. I do hope none of them have been injured."

"Keep in mind," Dun Scotus commented, "the stairs I proposed would serve them as well. If there were such a thing in place now, the Celtar could descend to the safety of the Great Hall without having to fly out in this dangerous wind and rain."

This gave the Blackwellers pause. Perhaps a staircase to Strongbeak Loft would be a worth while undertaking after all. As Dun Scotus had pointed out, he'd come to Blackwell to offer his advice on improving the Abbey's defenses. They'd have to give serious consideration to his proposal, and make a decision only after they'd discussed it thoroughly amongst themselves. That was the Blackwell way. Outside, the fierce summer storm raged on.

CHAPTER 6

The rain kept up all night, and showed no signs of abating as the gray, soggy summer morning broke over Primley.

A somber breakfast was taken in the Great Hall, followed a few hours later by an even more somber lunch. No beast could remember the last time it had rained so hard for so long. There was much concern that the gardens might suffer damage from the prolonged deluge with its high winds, and that crops would be lost.

It was hardest for the Abbey children, for whom not being able to go outside was just about the worst punishment that nature could have provided. Neo certainly had her paws full that day; when she wasn't traversing the tunnels to the bell tower and climbing the stairs to sound the dreary day's various tollings, she was chasing around after restless young-beasts who were trying to have the hallowed halls of Blackwell make do for the open outside places they couldn't go.

Come evening, every beast gathered in the Great Hall for their second rain-bound supper in as many nights. The main course was supplied by the moles. Since the nasty weather was keeping them from their usual grounds work and they had so much time on their heavy digging claws, they'd descended upon Friar Calgarus's kitchens and spent all afternoon cooking up a trio of their famous deeper 'n' ever vegetable pies.

When every beast sat down around the dinner tables, Foremole made a special point of seating himself near Lord Scotus and piling up the Badger Lord's plate personally.

"'ere y'go, zurr," Hollnow said, dishing out a portion to Dun Scotus that even Gorver might have choked upon, "noice 'n' 'ot, jus' ee way et's s'posed t'be, not loik ee left overs you'm 'ad two noights ago. Oi'm shure you'm loik et, zurr."

"My thanks," Dun Scotus nodded, seeming to have no difficulty understanding the rustic molespeech. He took the plate and proceeded to tuck into the steaming, gravy-oozing slice of pie. Seeing that, their honored guest had been properly served, the others dove in themselves ... Graupuss almost literally.

As the meal went on, Brae and Skara made conversation by asking Dun Scotus how he was enjoying his stay at Blackwell.

"Your hospitality is of course without fault," the badger warrior rumbled amiably, "but I am not here to enjoy myself. After this meal, before the daylight fails altogether, I should want to go out to tour the grounds and visit the wall top."

Every beast within hearing of this statement was dumbfounded. Brae and Skara traded a brows-raised glance, not sure they'd heard correctly. "Go outside?" the Abbess said. "In this weather?"

"A leader must be willing to endure the same hardships as those he commands. It would not be fair for your sentries to subject themselves to this rain unless we are willing to share their burden." Dun Scotus's eyes narrowed at the two mice. "You do have lookouts posted on the wall top, do you not?"

"At nearly all times," said Brae.

"But not today?"

"Today?" She laughed, incredulous. "My Lord, be reasonable! You can't expect a creature to stand guard out in a storm such as this."

"But that is precisely what I expect, Abbess. The enemies of peace travel by day and by night, in every kind of weather. If you have no beast standing watch right now, there could be an enemy horde assembled outside your gates at this very moment." The great badger heaved an exasperated sigh. "I have offered you my counsel in improving Blackwell's defenses. Once again, I find the security of this Abbey wanting."

Gorver, Vondick and old Graupulous joined Brae and Skara in staring at Dun Scotus in stunned silence. "Now, My Lord," Graupulous said, "I hardly think you're being fair... "

"Fair?" Dun Scotus lanced each of them in turn with his gaze of steel. "I came to Blackwell to warn you of a crisis that could break upon us at any moment and throw the lands into greater tumolt than any they have ever known. What must I say or do to convince you to take my prophecy seriously?"

An abashed silence met his question. Both Brae and Graupulous felt they ought to protest Dun Scotus's harsh assessment. But how could they, when he had offered to venture out into the wind and rain himself for their benefit? If this seasoned warrior saw need for such a thing, then who were they - who had never known war in their lifetimes - to naysay him?

Gorver jumped into the awkward silence, shattering it with his ebullient manner. "Aw, nothin' t' get our rudders all outta whack about, is there? This badger fella's right, an' that's all there is to it. Soon as I'm finished tuckin' inta this tuck, Terious an' me'll get t'gether an' knock out a sentry duty rotation fer every beast at Blackwell, so's we can have wall top lookouts at all times. Me 'n' me otters can take th' watches in rough seas like this since a liddle rain don't bother us one flick of a whisker. Ain't that right, Brady lad?"

Grauparus, seated at an adjacent table, looked uncertain. "Um, but I'm helping Brother Skara down in the archives, Graupuss sir."

"Huh? Oh, well, o' course you are! You will be excused since yore helpin' get us ready fer this great crisis in yer own way. But the rest o' us waterdogs will be out standin' our first watch before darkness falls. An' then Terious an' his squirrels can take over when the rain clears up. Ain't that so, Terious matey?"

"Uh, sure, Graupuss." Vondick could not work up the enthusiasm to match his longtime companions. Like most of the other Blackwell leaders around the tables, he was still stinging from Dun Scotus's criticism of the Abbey's preparedness, more so since he was the chief of the Primley Patrol. As such was largely responsible for keeping the security not only of Blackwell, but this entire region.

Dun Scotus abruptly changed subject, saying to Brae, "Have you reached any decision yet about my proposal for that staircase up to Strongbeak Loft?"

"Uh, no, we haven't, My Lord. We haven't had a chance to consult with the Celtar yet. We'll do so, as soon as it stops raining."

She glanced up toward the stained glass windows, where the heavy drops still spattered loudly against the multi-hued panes, creating a ceaseless back ground drumming throughout the Great Hall.

"If it ever does," she added, almost to herself.

The rain continued to fall through the night, and the second straight dismal morning dawned over Blackwell and Primley Woods. Breakfast was a gloomy affair in spite of the extra torches and the plentitude of hot, fresh, aromatic breads and cakes. It was as if the very forces of nature were conspiring to cast a dark mantle of doom over Blackwell, and dampen the spirit of the Abbey itself.

Not even Gorver was on paw to lighten the mood. True to his word, he and Vondick had devised a sentry schedule after the previous night's dinner. Afterwards, he and his otters had begun taking the first of their soggy watches. But Blackwell was home to relatively few otters, the only creatures designed for standing guard in heavy rain. Most of them were either still out on the wall top or resting from the shift they'd put in overnight. Graupuss was never a beast to miss a meal, and the fact that he was absent from breakfast showed that Lord Scotus's criticism had stung him far more than his out ward joviality let on.

The Abbey lawns were thoroughly sodden from the two solid days of rain, and large muddy puddles had formed throughout the orchard. The pond had risen far above its banks and flooded well onto the lawns, much to the delight of the fish and shrimp who lived in it. But it was the state of the gardens that was most worry some, for that was where the Abbey got much of its food. Some of the crop was sure to have been destroyed, in spite of the protective measures that had been taken just before the storm hits.

Just as some of the woodlanders began to think they would never see the sun again, the rain slacked off and the clouds thinned. Shortly before lunchtime, patches of glorious blue sky could be seen through the clouds over Primley, and shifting shafts of sunlight stabbed down across the dark forest canopy. Up on the ramparts, Graupuss and his otters were rewarded for their long and soggy vigil by the sight of a rainbow arching high above the Abbey.

It flickered and shimmered in and out of existence for some moments, then the brightening sunlight solidified it into a spectral display of wondrous proportions. The sight raised a hearty cheer from Graupuss's crew.

In his room on the top dormitory floor, Dun Scotus glanced up from the Abbey chronicle he was reading and looked out the window to see the last shredded vestiges of the storm racing westward, toward Astapailia and the open sea.

Soon the lawns were full of rejoicing Blackwellers, adults as unabashed in their glee as were the young ones. Paws and sandals quickly grew wet and muddy, but no beast could care about that when the sunny, blue, rainbow-crossed sky was to be seen above. Neo rushed to ring the bells to announce both the midday meal and the end of the storm.

The only creatures at Blackwell not immediately aware of this change for the better were the four toiling away in a tunnel end deep below the Abbey, delving into the past for some possible clue to Blackwell's future...

Serius sneezed..again.

Syril glanced aside at his younger brother. "Nice catch, Se."

"Uh, thanks." Serius finished wiping his snout and replaced his kerchief in his habit pocket. He left one corner sticking out so he could produce it again in a hurry should another sneeze come upon him ... as it no doubt would before too long.

Brother Skara and Grauparus the otter watched the explosive nasal display long enough to satisfy themselves that their youngest helper hadn't soiled any of the Abbey records, then went back to reading their own chronicles.

Syril sat resting his chin in one paw while he twirled a dry stylus in the other. This was their third day down in the Abbey archives, and the novelty of the project had long since worn off for the older mouse brother.

Syril had expected some great treasury of tales to be opened to him, some passage to world that would excite his newfound interest in warrior matters. Instead, the Abbey chronicles had turned out to be mostly a record of the unextraordinary. Blackwell had known peace for nearly all its long history. The records were an endless list of routine births and passings, observations on the weather, marriages, changes of Seasons, celebrations, notes on visitors to the Abbey ... every detail of the hum-drum comings and goings of the most unexceptional of creatures. In short, life at Blackwell in the past had been, with few exceptions, very much as it was today.

This disappointing discovery had sent Syril into a spiral of boredom. He would have asked Skara to excuse him from this chore, if he weren't afraid of offending the historian.

It wouldn't have been so bad if they'd uncovered at least some small clue of what they were looking for, but so far they had found nothing. Three days of effort had barely scratched the surface of these vast archives.

There were enough documents here to keep all four of them searching for seasons! It also didn't help knowing that the weather up above ground was so gloomy and depressing. Even though the archive tunnel was totally shut off from the world out-side, the lingering storm seemed to have reached down into the chamber, making its enclosed spaces seem more oppressive. Every time one of them ventured up to the Great Hall or to the dormitories, only to be met by more of the clouds and rain that made it all the harder to return to the confines of the archives where the sun never shone. It was like they brought a little bit of the storm back with them each time, weighing down the mood even more.

It never occurred to Syril that Brother Skara and Grauparus - and perhaps even his own brother Serius - were truly engrossed in their inspection of the histories, and were not feeling the kind of restlessness that he was.

Syril's openly listless attitude did not go unnoticed by Skara. The historian glanced up, peering over the top of his spectacles at the young mouse for the dozenth time that morning.

"I say, Syril, have you actually read a single word of that record yet? You've been on that page for so long, it's starting to collect dust."

Syril's chin slipped from his paw upon hearing his name, and he had to scramble to keep his balance.

"Huh? Oh, I was just thinking, Mr. Skara."

"Gatherin' some wool, more like it," Grauparus put in with a chuckle. "Been guilty of doin' that myself a time or three."

Syril continued playing absently with the stylus, looking at, but not really seeing the page before him.

"These records are just the same things over and over again. Who cares what some beast had for dinner twenty generations ago?"

"This is our history, Syril," said Skara. "Our heritage. Everything Blackwell stands for is to be found here."

"But it's not why we're doing this," Syril retorted. "We're supposed to be looking for clues about some war that's coming, and we haven't found anything like that and, we've barely begun to read what's here!"

"We knew this would be a formidable task when we started," Skara reminded Syril. "That's why I asked you and Serius and Grauparus to assist me. Imagine how long it would take if I had to do this alone."

Grauparus nodded knowingly. "Patience is a virtue."

"There's no need to be trite," Syril muttered under his breath.

Skara's ears were sharper than his eyes, and immediately his brow furrowed angrily. "And there's no need to be rude. Now, apologize to Grauparus this instant!"

Syril hung his head. "Sorry, Brady."

Skara took a deep breath, shaking his head as he exhaled. "First, all that talk about wanting to become a warrior, and now this! What's come over you these days, Syril?"

Syril didn't answer. Before Skara could berate him further, Serius frantically snatched for his kerchief and uncorked another impressive sneeze, with barely enough time to turn his head and cover his face.

"Caught that 'un too, Syr," he said impishly. "Ooo, this drydust is really tickling my poor nose. I'll never stop sneezing."

Grauparus leaned over and whispered into Skara's ear, "Looks like one of our assistant's soured to this task, and the other's in discomfort. P'raps we should let these two mousies return to their bellringin' duties an' find some other beasts to help us read these records?"

Skara considered the young otter's advice. "Perhaps," he said out loud. "But I tend to think it's this weather that's gotten us down, even down here, so to speak. No beast I've talked to can remember a storm like this, and it's weighed upon the spirit of every beast at Blackwell.

It must be hard on these two youngsters, so full of energy, to spend hours down here in this tunnel, only to go upstairs and find the day as sunless and depressing as the darkest cellar."

He marked his spot and closed the book before him. "I think maybe we should take a rest from this task until the storm passes and the sun returns, and then we can take some of these records up and read them out on the lawns in the sunlight. Some of these books haven't seen the light of day in many generations, and it won't do them or us any harm."

"That might be awhile," Grauparus ventured. "This storm's shapin' up to be a classic."

"Oh, it's got to end sometime. It can't keep up like this very much longer," Skara said optimistically. "Even if it takes another day or two, the sun will return over Primley as surely as the spirit of Septimus watches over every beast at Blackwell."

Barely had these words passed Skara's lips than there came a bustling from the main tunnel. It was Rufus, and the young mole seemed unusually cheerful.

"Burr hurr, zurrs! yrull, Seriuz! Ee sun be a-shoinin' agin at last! Cum upp'n 'ave a gudd lunch out-soide, gennel beasts!"

"Well, well!" Skara stood. "See, one has only to speak the name of Septimus to improve one's fortunes! Let's all take good master Rufus's advice and have a good meal out of doors, and then we'll see about continuing our workout on the Abbey lawns. Good food and bright sun should be enough to improve all our dispositions."

The four archive searchers followed Rufus down the tunnel, hastening to be in the inviting summer sun once more.

CHAPTER 7

Lunch that day ended up being taken on the top of the wall since the lawns and orchard were still a wet mess from the rains.

There was little shade to be found up on the ramparts, but after the lengthy storm no beast minded a good dose of sun. A fresh breeze provided a balance to the strong sunshine, and helped dry the wall top walk-way while the Abbey grounds below still lay in their drenched, dripping, sun-bejewelled splendor. It had turned into the kind of day that made a creature glad to be alive.

Skara, Grauparus, Syril, Serius and Rufus found a clear spot for themselves along the crowded ramparts. Nibbling at some white and yellow breaded cheese, Skara sniffed at the fresh, clean air while the breeze rippled the fur on the top of his head.

"Ah, glorious! Bit gusty, though. I wouldn't want to risk bringing any of the records up here until the wind calms down some - they might get blown away and, it's too wet down on the lawns. Perhaps we should plan on taking the rest of the day off, and get a fresh start tomorrow morning."

Abbess Brae was within earshot, escorting Lord Scotus along the wall top as they surveyed the surrounding countryside for damage from the storm.

"Hello, Skara. How is your search of the archives going?"

"Oh, hello, Brae. Lord Scotus," Skara nodded as the two approached. "Well, it's fascinating reading, but we haven't really found anything of use yet, as far as Lord Scotus's prophecy is concerned. Our young assistants were getting a bit antsy. This wall top lunch was just the break we needed."

"Yes, it is grand to have the sun shining again," Brae readily agreed. "Do you think you might need more of us to help you with your reading?"

"It might come to that." Skara removed his spectacles from the end of his snout and pinched at the bridge of his nose. "I tell you, it doesn't help that my eyes aren't as young as they used to be, or that Blackwell hasn't had a decent lens crafter in many a season. I've even tried my own paw at the grinding and polishing wheels, but no beast among us has the gift with glass to become a truly skilled lens-maker. A really fine pair of reading spectacles would help greatly, but I'll have to make do with these."

Dun Scotus stepped forward, holding out a paw. "May I?"

Skara was surprised. "Oh ... of course." He passed his glasses to the Badger Lord. Dun Scotus scrutinized them carefully, holding them up to the sun and turning them about under his gaze.

"Yes, a bit on the crude side. Serviceable, I'm sure, but a true master of the craft could do much better. I know some beasts up north who could improve upon this."

"Really?" Brae remarked. The Northlands had such a reputation as a wild and warlike region, it was easy to forget that there must be many honest and decent creatures living there as well ... crafts beasts among them. "Well, Lord, if any of them would care to bring their skills to Blackwell, I can guarantee they would never want for a bed or three meals a day ... not to mention our deepest gratitude."

"I will make inquiries, next time I am up north." Dun Scotus stood staring at Skara's glasses, held delicately in his giant paw. "This reminds me of something I saw once. Some children were out playing on a sunny day. They'd found a magnifying glass that belonged to their parents. They discovered that if they held it up to the sun in just the right way," and now Dun Scotus angled Skara's spectacles until two brilliant white crescents appeared on the rampart stone work, "that they could generate a burning heat. They were using the glass to burn small insects."

"That's cruel!" Skara and Brae blurted out as one.

Dun Scotus made no comment on their out cry, but continued to gaze at the pair of reading glasses. "A warrior going into battle must always consider the sun. Whether it is in his eyes or his enemy's can make the difference between victory and defeat, as even non-fighting beasts know. But ever since that day, I have wondered whether the sun could be used as an actual weapon.

With lenses and perhaps mirrors of the proper size, might not a device be made which could focus sunlight just as these do, but on a scale that could incinerate an approaching army before it ever drew within arrow range?"

Brae gave a sharp intake of breath as she envisioned the horror of such a scene.

Skara chuckled uneasily, convinced that Scotus must surely be joking. "You would need pretty big lenses and mirrors, My Lord."

"And it wouldn't work on a cloudy day," Syril added.

Dun Scotus's gaze shot down toward the young mouse, seated a short distance away. "A very astute observation. You have spotted the primary weakness to such a weapon. You truly do show the tactical sharpness of a warrior and, perhaps a captain at that."

Syril grinned widely at this compliment from a seasoned fighter, but Skara was quick to quash the elation.

"Well, no beast here will be building such a thing, if it could be built at all, which I doubt. As for my young helper here, I'm afraid that all this warrior talk has been having a detrimental effect on Syril. Lately he's seemed restless and inattentive and, today he made a discourteous remark to Grauparus. Hardly the proper young bellringer I know."

Brae arched an eyebrow toward Syril. "Oh, really?"

Grauparus nodded. "'fraid so, Abbess."

Syril hung his head and tried to make himself invisible.

"Well, well," Brae clucked, "I think you'd better sit this young one down for a good long talk ... not about fanciful dreams of war, but more important things, like respect for his elders."

Syril looked up at Brae. "But, Mother Abbess ... someday Blackwell will need a new warrior champion. Who is it going to be?"

"Right now, it appears Gorver has appointed himself to that post," Brae chuckled.

"I've seen him walking around lately with the sword of Septimus strapped to his waist. No harm in that, I suppose, as long as he doesn't go swimming with it on!" Dun Scotus returned Skara's spectacles to the recorder mouse. "I have more reading to do before the evening meal. If you good beasts will excuse me ... "He turned and descended the nearby wall stairs to the lawns below.

Skara balanced his glasses back on the tip of his nose. "Using lenses to burn creatures! Imagine! Do you suppose such a thing could be done, Brae?"

The Abbess was watching Dun Scotus retreating figure. "I just do believe that if any-beast could achieve such a thing that badger would be the one to do it."

After lunch, Syril and Serius went with Neo across the wet lawns and up into the bell tower. Now that it had finally stopped raining, the Abbess wanted to consult with the Celtar about Dun Scotus's proposal for a stairway up to Strongbeak Loft.

Neo was not skilled enough on the bells to be sure she could properly summon a Celtar messenger down from their court. The mouse brothers were more than happy to have a brief return to their old duties up in the airy belfrey after their days down in the dark archives. Neo watched attentively as they tolled out the correct sequence on the Maximus and Neltron bells.

When they were finished, the three of them joined others who had gathered at the foot of the tower. Looking skyward, they saw two birds emerge from the eaves of Strongbeak Loft and circle down toward them.

One of the birds turned out to be Pirphor, Grauparus's young Celtra friend. The otter assumed a playful boxing stance and dealt his sparrow sparring partner a soft tap on the beak.

"Pirphor, y'old featherbag! Thought you were blown away in that storm!"

"No such luckee for you, waterdog!" Pirphor flapped his wings at Grauparus.

The other Celtar was their leader, Strongwing. The older bird gave Grauparus and Pirphor a sour look. "Ah, the foolishness of youth!"

"Yes," Brae grinned, "just like you and Graupuss used to kibbitz around when you were that age. And, correct me if I'm wrong, but aren't you the very creature who invented the idea of otter/Celtar sparring?"

"Ahem. Yes, perhaps. But Graupuss and I were always more dignified about it than those two."

"Oh, yes. Whatever you say." Brae and Strongwing were the closest of friends, and were not above casting a few jibes each other's way. "But seriously, how are things up in Strongbeak Loft? That was a vicious storm. Did you suffer any damage or injuries up there?"

"A few wet nests, nothing more. Although we are all quite peckish, no pun intended. We weren't able to forage for food during the strom, and there wasn't much reserve food around the Loft. This young fool Pirphor almost risked flying down in the rain to ask you for something from your kitchens, but in the end we all decided to sit tight until the storm passed. Most of the Celtar are out in Primley right now, filling their bellies and digging up some worms and such to bring back for our nestlings." Brae suppressed a pang of queasiness. The food preferences of most Celtar were not to the taste of everybeast. Strongwing himself had been raised in the lower Abbey by the woodlanders, and so did not fully share the eating habits of his fellow birds. He was, in truth, quite proud of the fact that he'd never actually eaten a worm, and was probably the only sparrow in all of Primley who could make such a claim, or would even want to.

"Well, I'm glad things went well for you during the storm, all things considered. The main reason I called you down was to discuss a certain matter with you." Brae explained about Dun Scotus's proposal for the Great Hall stairway to Strongbeak Loft.

"Well," she concluded, "what do you think, my friend?"

"I think it's a capital idea, if it can be done," Strongwing said with enthusiasm. "We Celtar may tend to go our own way most of the time, but when it comes right down to it, we are Blackwellers all the same. An easy way for us to visit each other could only solidify our friendship."

"Hollnow thinks it's possible to build it, although it would of course be a great undertaking and there's no way to guess how long it would take to complete. Go talk it over with the other Celtar, and if there are no objections ... well, then I suppose there's no reason we can't start on it right away."

"I'll convene a full wing meet this evening after every bird returns from foraging, and then drop by tomorrow with our answer. I honestly anticipate no problem - I think this is an idea every Celtar will support."

The eloquent sparrow spread his wings to fly off, but before he could become air born, Neo called him back.

"One more thing, Strongwing," the badger matriarch said. "Since Syril and Serius, our usual bellringers, are helping Skara with his special project down in the archives, I'll be in charge of the bells for a while."

Strongwing cocked his head at her. "So that explains that racket we heard down here just before the storm. We figured it was supposed to be a storm warning. Either that, or some beast had gone mad and was trying to end it all by strangling itself on the bell ropes."

"Very funny. Anyway, they will be showing me the different tolls now, so you will be hearing a lot of ringing for the next hour or so. Don't pay any attention to it - it won't mean we're trying to summon you."

Brae furrowed her brow. "But, Neo ... what if something does happen while you're practicing on the bells that does require us to alert the Celtar? What will we do then?"

"No problem that," Pirphor cawed, pausing in his horseplay with Grauparus. "I stay down here with pal waterdog, until big stripedogmum finish bellsounds. Any trouble, I fly up Strongbeak Loft, bring Strongwing."

"A workable plan," Strongwing agreed. "Very well, then. I'll bid all you good beasts a pleasant afternoon, and speak with you again on the morrow." He flapped away, climbing the fresh breeze back up to the high roof of Blackwell.

"What a well-spoken bird," Neo said in admiration.

"Yes," Brae nodded. "His upbringing in the lower Abbey certainly helped him in that regard. Too bad he couldn't teach more of the Celtar to speak like that."

"A losing cause, I think," said Neo. "Trying to teach eloquence to sparrows, of all creatures! Must frustrate the dickens out of him."

Pirphor was hanging on the outer fringe of their conversation. "Hey!" he protested. "What wrong with way Celtar speak!"

"Oh ... nothing. Nothing at all," Brae assured him, then turned her head to hide her amused chuckle.

That evening, while most Blackwellers were finishing up their light-hearted supper in the stained glass splendor of the Great Hall, Brother Zulu paid a visit to the Infirmary.

Sister Juliett looked up from her back corner desk upon the recorder mouse's arrival. "Hello, Brother Zulu! Is anything the matter?"

"I was about to make the same inquiry of you," Zulu chuckled. "You've certainly been making yourself scare these past few days. One would hardly know this Abbey even has an Infirmary keeper!"

"And how would you know?" Juliett challenged. "Spending all your time down in those dusty old tunnels!"

"I do make it up for meals and bedtime," he said. "But that was the very reason I came to see you - that drying powder of the moles in the archives is giving all of us scratchy throats. I was wondering if you could spare a few of those herbal candies you specialize in."

"What, and not some nice hot nettle broth? That's so much better for sore throats ... "

Skara held up both paws. "Please, no. Your hard suckers taste so much nicer!"

"I knew you'd say that. Very well ... "Juliett dug into one side drawer of her small desk and produced of small cloth bag of the desired candies. "Here you go. That's the last of them. Looks like I'll have to whip up some more, when I get the chance."

Skara glanced around the deserted Infirmary as he took the bag from her. "Doesn't look like you have much to keep you from that right now."

"Yes, we Blackwellers are healthy as hogs just at the moment and you won't hear me complaining about it one bit!"

"So, if that's the case, why are you keeping such a low profile these days?"

Sister Juliett glanced left and right, as if afraid some beast might have materialized out of thin air to eavesdrop on them. "Well, if you must know, it's that badger. I've been trying to avoid him."

Skara was intrigued. "Really? Why is that?"

She told him all about her unnerving encounter with Dun Scotus on the badger's first night at Blackwell. Skara had of course heard about the incident since Juliett had shared the experience with Friar Calgarus and Ularus the following morning, but this was his first time hearing the tale related by the mouse-maid herself.

"I know I must sound like a silly young mouse," she concluded, "but if you'd been there ... "Juliett shook her head. "It's hard to find the right words to explain what it was like."

Skara mulled it over. "Actually, I think I know just what you're trying to say. It's like ... well, like Lord Scotus doesn't belong at Blackwell."

"Exactly and, not just because he's such a grim warrior. Blackwell has hosted Badger Lords before him, and we've had warrior champions of our own. Dun Scotus, on the other paw ... well, there's just something about him that makes my fur crawl."

Skara sighed. "You're not the only beast who feels that way. Just this afternoon, up on the wall, he was going on about building some kind of weapon out of giant lenses and mirrors, to burn opposing armies with sunlight."

He waited for Juliett to join him in his uneasy laughter at the outlandish idea, but she merely stared at him blank faced and said, "I don't doubt for one moment that that badger would build such a device if he could and, that he would not hesitate to use it."

Skara shuddered at this confirmation of his own opinions about the brooding badger warrior. "Well, let me tell you, I feel I've had enough of Dun Scotus's company to last me a season. That conversation we had this afternoon un-nerved me, same as you must have been on that first night."

"There's just something ... un-natural ... about that badger, Lord or no. Maybe supernatural is more like it and, the way he's been storming around the place, I'm surprised he hasn't staged a surprise inspection of the Infirmary ... tried to install some battlements in here to defend the sick, or something like that."

"Yes, he does seem to be putting Blackwell on a war footing," Skara agreed. "All ready for war ... but not an enemy in sight."

Sister Juliett threw up her paws. "I know it's improper to talk like this about an honored guest of Blackwell, especially one who's come to help us, but ... well, I just hope Lord Scotus stays healthy while he's here because if I had to treat him as a patient for any length of time, I honestly don't know whether I could do it."

She stared at Skara. "You won't tell any beast about what I said here, will you? I can't help the way I feel about Dun Scotus, but I'd hate to have it get back to him."

"Oh, I don't know ... I think he might be flattered to learn what an impression he's made on both of us." Seeing Juliett's brow furrow with concern, Skara laughed. "Don't worry. I don't want him finding that out any more than you do." He turned and headed for the door, thanking Juliett again for the cough drops.

Brother Marko, Blackwell's chief horticulturalist, escorted Abbess Brae up and down the rows of the gardens, conducting her on a tour of the ruination the storm had caused.

"All the grain and cereal crops were flattened," Marko was saying. "Wheat, oat, corn, barley ... all a total loss."

"Well, we can always mill acorns and other nuts to get flour from them," said Brae, "and we can gather as many of those as we need from the woods. What else?"

"The leafy greens were also a total loss. Lettuce, fennel, parsley, celery, spinach ... "Brother Marko sighed. "The good news is that it's still early enough in the growing season to plant another crop of those. Same with the herbs and spices, although Friar Calgarus says we have a good supply of those in dried form in the kitchens. The flower gardens, on the other paw, will take until next spring to recover. We'll have to make do without scented water for the next couple of seasons, and our supplies of honey may run low by winter's end, unless our bees fly far afield to gather wild nectar."

"What about the rest?" Brae inquired.

"The underground vegetables seem to be all right. As long as the wetness in the soil doesn't start an out-break of root rot, our crops of carrots, potatoes, turnips and beets should be as plentiful as ever. As far as the berry vines go, about half the harvest was lost. But that should still give us all we'll need until next year."

"And the orchards?"

"Hollnow and I gave them a thorough inspection earlier this morning, Abbess. The damage there seems light. If we use fruit from the trees for the next two sea-sons' batches of cordials, we can save the surviving berries for pastries, preserves and jams. It should all balance out."

Brae paused, lifting her face to the morning sun. The cool breeze that had ushered out the storm had diminished, letting the usual summer heat settle back in over Primley country. Looking up at the cloudless blue sky, it was hard to believe that such a savage blast of weather had visited them so recently. Only the squishy soil of the garden under her bare paws gave testament to the copious amounts of rain that had fallen.

Teams of moles worked all around them, crouched low with their snouts to the ground as they pulled up ruined plants. Of all creatures, they could best sense which plants were beyond repair and which could be salvaged, especially with the tubered varieties such as carrots and beets. It was on their say so that Brother Marko had pronounced those crops healthy.

Brae breathed deeply of the earth-fragrant air. "Well, it could have been a lot worse, all things considered. These losses will be an inconvenience, but they won't result in any serious shortages of food. Mostly it will be a matter doing without some of the luxuries we are used to, but we'll be fine on the basics."

Some beast called out to her. Brae glanced around at Brother Marko and the moles before realizing that the voice had come from above. Strongwing dropped out of the sky three paces from her, rebounding lightly from his landing on the soft garden humus.

"Ahh, good morning, Abbess!" the Celtar leader greeted her boisterously. "How are you this fine summer day?"

"Getting my paws all muddied in the course of my Abbess's duties," she joked. "Just looking over the damage to the gardens. Bad, but not too bad. How goes it with you, my friend?"

Strongwing bobbed his head in customary sparrow fashion. "I just wanted to let you know that I spoke with all the Celtar last evening, on the subject of those stairs Lord Scotus wants to build up to Strongbeak Loft. There was very little debate, miracle of miracles. Nearly every Celtar thinks it would be a wonderful thing to have. We'll even help build it, if there's any way at all that we can be of assistance."

"Why, thank you for your offer, Strongwing. Go speak with Hollnow, he's around here some place ... oh, there he is, over by the Noles, or what used to be the Noles before the storm. He can tell you better than myself what will be involved in building those stairs, and how you might be able to help. Now that you Celtar have approved the project, I guess we'll be getting right on it."

Strongwing bobbed-bowed his head and bade her good day, then hopped across the garden rows to where Hollnow knelt.

"Careful with those talons, sir!" Brother Marko cried out at the sparrow. "Some of those crops are still good!"

Brae chuckled and strode out of the cultivated garden plots and onto the Abbey lawn. No sooner had she left Brother Marko's side than she heard her name being called yet again.

She turned to see Ularus rounding the corner of the Abbey building and hastening toward her as fast as her short hedgehog legs would carry her. The cellar-keeper was clearly agitated, waving her arms wildly as she drew near.

"Brae, you'd best come quick! That badger's at it again!"

The Abbess regarded Ularus with both concern and sternness. "Do You mean Lord Scotus? What's that supposed to mean, 'at it again?' That's no way to talk about a guest of Blackwell."

Ularus shrugged. "Guest or no, I think Vondick is about to murder that brute."

"What?"

"It's over another of 'is lordship's wonderful ideas. Come with me, an' yer'll see what I mean." Ularus turned and ran back the way she'd come.

Brae gave a resigned sigh and glanced downward. Both her footpaws and the hem of her habit were muddy from her tour of the gardens, and she'd have to go attend to their honored guest with no chance to get cleaned up first. Oh, well, Lord Scotus had surely seen worse in the Northlands. Brae hurried after Ularus to see what all the fuss was about.

"No! I won't let you!"

Vondick stood before Dun Scotus on the south lawns, paws on his hips in a stance of open defiance toward the badger warrior. Woody and several other squirrels of the Primley Patrol stood behind him in a show of support. Vondick's bushy tail twitched like an angry snake, betraying the full depth of his agitation.

Dun Scotus regarded Vondick with his usual coolness. "That is not your decision to make, but the Abbess's and, here she is now."

It was a tense scene that greeted Brae when she arrived, with Ularus jogging at her side. She'd heard Vondick's angry shouts from clear across the Abbey grounds. Brother Skara, Syril, Serius and Grauparus had paused in their readings of the histories up on the battlements, and stood gazing down at the confrontation between squirrel and badger. Gorver's attention had also been drawn by the shouting, and he'd raced over from the pond with several other otters to try to help calm the situation.

"What is going on here?" Brae demanded with utmost authority.

Vondick pointed accusingly at Dun Scotus. "He wants to cut down the trees!"

Brae was confused. She glanced over at the orchard, which contained the only trees within Blackwell, then back at Terious. "What trees? What are you talking about?"

Dun Scotus pointed to the east wall, and the high oaks and elms that towered over the wall top. It was at that spot that Primley Woods came closest to the Abbey. "Those trees, Abbess. They pose a hazard."

"Oh?" Brae understood now why Vondick was so upset. The squirrels often used those tall trees as a short cut into Blackwell, leaping nimbly from the higher branches onto the wall top when they didn't feel like waiting for some beast to open one of the wall gates to admit them. No creature, but a squirrel would dare to use such a way in and out of the Abbey. Brae herself often frowned upon such activity. But Terious and his squirrels were natural climbers, and since none had ever slipped and fallen during all the seasons Terious had headed the Primley Patrol, she turned a blind eye to their dizzying jumps. If those trees were cut down, it would put a permanent end to their acrobatic shortcuts, and they'd be forced to use the gates like every beast else.

Brae waved a paw for Terious to be quiet. "Please explain this, My Lord. What kind of hazard do you believe they pose?"

"I have been reading your histories, Abbess. During the war with Teivel the Terrible, and again during Blackwell's conflict with the Wayfoxes, enemies of this Abbey nearly succeeded in using those trees to climb over the wall and breach your defenses. On those occasions, it was only luck which prevented total catastrophe. If it almost worked for them, it will work for others. Those trees must come down, for the safety of Blackwell."

Vondick could hold his silence no longer. "If you've read those histories," he snapped at Dun Scotus, "then you will also know that those trees were used to get Maximus safely back into Blackwell when he was lost in Primley. Squirrels have often come and gone by that route when the territory outside the walls have been occupied by enemies and impassible to any ground creature. Those trees have done Blackwell far more good than harm over the seasons."

"Vondick makes good points," Brae said, "and here are some more. We here at Blackwell are loathe to cut down any tree unnecessarily. Whenever possible, we take our firewood from dead branches and logs from the forest floor, or from trees that are sick or dying. We only cut down healthy trees when we need solid, dependable lumber for building ... and then we are ever mindful to plant new saplings to take their place in the seasons to come. You speak of our security, My Lord. Thanks to you, we have full-time sentries in place on the wall top now. No enemy of Blackwell could breach our walls in the manner you suggest, now that we have increased our watchfulness. Besides, the only creatures who could easily use that way into Blackwell without special devices are squirrels, and they are not enemies."

"Not all tree climbers are friendly," Dun Scotus countered in his smooth rumble. "There are tribes of tree rats even here in Primley and, remember the Painted Ones your champion Maximus encountered on his way to Tacitus to retrieve his stolen son from slavers ... "

"Skara's right. You do know our history surprisingly well," Brae admitted. "But the Painted Ones lived many days' march to the south, atop the high cliff wall from which there's no easy way down. They pose no threat to Blackwell."

"Maximus made it up that cliff, and back down again," Dun Scotus reminded her. " In times of upheaval and crisis, enemies and allies alike may be displaced and suddenly turn up where you would not expect to find them and, there may be others like the Painted Ones, not yet known to us. It would be unfortunate to learn of them only when they swarm over these walls in a massed assault."

"Yes, that would be terrible indeed," said Brae, the barest hint of sarcasm in her tone. "But Vondick and his squirrels range far and wide throughout these woods, gathering news from the farthest fringes of Primley. They would know of any such enemies, and whether they were planning an attack, long before they reached Blackwell."

"Oh? and, tell me, exactly how many patrols have they made in the time I have been at Blackwell?"

This unexpected question set Terious stammering. "But, but first it was a celebration day, and then the storm for two days ... "

"Ah," Dun Scotus nodded, "so the answer is none. Abbess, if I could demonstrate to you that a large horde might be able to come upon this Abbey without any advance warning, avoiding the notice of even your squirrel patrols, would you then consent to have those trees cut down?"

Brae considered this. "You would have to make your case most convincingly, My Lord. What exactly did you have in mind?"

"Oh, I was speaking hypothetically. Perhaps an opportunity to provide such a demonstration will arise before the time comes for me to leave Blackwell. If not, you will of course have to do what you think best for this Abbey."

"Of course."Brae perked up. "On a lighter note, My Lord, the Celtar met last night to discuss your idea of a stairway up to Strongbeak Loft, and they think it would be a fine thing. Hollnow will start making the preparations to build it. I'm sure he will want to consult with you on the design, and take another look at that sketch you made."

"I've since done an improved version," Dun Scotus informed her. "I'm sure he will want to see it."

"He's over in the gardens ... why not go speak with him now? The mole teams inspecting the crops can certainly spare him for something like this."

"Thank you, Abbess." Dun Scotus took his leave of them, strolling toward the gardens.

Vondick's tail was still twitching. "Dranda, you're not going to let him ... "

"Don't worry, Terious. No beast will be cutting down those trees any time soon. But you ought not to have gotten so excited. Lord Scotus is our guest. The next time you take issue with one of his suggestions, please try to be more civil about it."

Graupuss slapped his squirrel friend on the back. "Dranda's right 'bout that, Terious matey. I haven't seen yer brush twitch like that in a saucerful o' seasons! Ain't th' proper attitude t' show an ally, not even one like that 'un."

"Sorry. I just couldn't help myself. When he started talking about cutting down the trees ... "Terious gazed after the departing Badger Lord. "He's just so warlike, some-times I can't believe he's for real."

"All those seasons in the Northlands have made him a grim beast," Brae agreed. " And the weight of his prophecy can't be easy to bear. These are things we must keep in mind. But as long as he does nothing to violate our basic rules or upset our way of life, we must consider him friend, ally and honored guest of Blackwell. He is a Badger Lord of the mountain, after all."

"Yes, I suppose you're right, Brae," said Vondick. "I'll try not to let anything like that happen again."

The small crowd broke up, Blackwellers returning to their routine tasks. Up on the wall top, Skara and his fellow archive searchers returned their attention to their books, scrolls and parchments.

Brae found herself standing alone on the south lawn. Fighting the temptation to just fall onto her back for a nap in the warm summer sun, she hastened inside to wash up and change into a new habit, before another crisis arose and she had to face anybeast else in her garden-soiled state.

CHAPTER 8

Seeing that Serius had begun sniffling, Skara glanced up from his page and looked across the ramparts to the young mouse.

"Serius, is that dust still bothering you? I thought moving outdoors would solve that problem."

"Oh, it's not that, Mr. Nathan, sir." Serius pawed away a tear. "I jus' finished reading about the Battle of Bramwall that Septimus the Warrior fought before coming to Primley. The way poor Bramstrake was killed, it was so sad!"

Syril regarded his younger brother without sympathy. "Aw, that was a long time ago, Cy. Don't cry like a baby over it."

Skara cast a reproving glance at Syril. "When that tale was first told to us in the time of Abbot Utermum, nearly every beast at Blackwell openly wept at its tragedy. Septimus himself never spoke of Bramstrake, or any of his adventures in the Northlands. The memories must have been too painful for him."

Serius sniffed again. "I wish she could have lived."

"Well, that's the funny thing about history," Skara said. "Look at it this way, Serius. If Martha had not been killed in the Battle of Bramwall, Septimus almost surely would have married her.

They'd probably have settled down in her home of Pedro, since Septimus had lost his family to searats and slavers, and had nowhere else to go. Well, if that had happened, then Septimus never would have traveled south to Primley, never would have helped the decent woodlanders here vanquish the wildcat tyrants and, Blackwell Abbey might very well have never been built. The paw of fate is apparent in these events. From the tragedy of Septimus's great loss came something of much greater good."

"Fate can be pretty cruel, then, I guess," Serius sniffled, wiping his nose with his habit sleeve.

"Oh, brother," Syril muttered scornfully.

Skara crossed his arms over his chest in disapproval. "And tell us, young master Syril, what is wrong with a good beast showing some emotion over a tragic tale?"

Syril lifted his chin defiantly. "A warrior would never cry."

Skara clucked his tongue. "For your information, our own Septimus is recorded to have shed many a tear when his beloved wife Sinead passed on and, he is held to be the greatest warrior Blackwell had since Septimus himself. In fact, some beasts believe Maximus was our founding warrior's reincarnation, as foretold by Septimus himself and, that is as true a warrior as you can get."

"I bet Lord Scotus would never cry," Syril said.

Skara stared hard at Syril.

"No," he said after several moments, "no, I don't believe he would. I have not heard that badger laugh once since his arrival at Blackwell ... I don't think I've even seen him so much as crack a smile in all the time he's been here. I cannot imagine what horrors he must have witnessed to have made him so grim. I fear his heart has become so hardened by his warrior's existence that he can no longer truly enjoy life. Or perhaps it has more to do with the prophecy he was given, of knowing that the fate of so many creatures may rest upon him. His spirit almost seems to have become that of a beast who no longer fully walks in the world we know. You do not want to be like him, Syril ... trust me, you do not."

Syril maintained his defiant look, but did not meet the gazes of Skara, Grauparus or Serius.

"Syril," Skara softened his tone, "I know Lord Scotus's presence has had an effect on you, starting the day he arrived. But it's just a young beast's fascination for something new and exciting ... not that I ever engaged in such fantasies, but then we never had a Badger Lord visit Primley in my youth. You must understand this. If Scotus were to leave tomorrow, you'd quickly forget all about these warlike matters and realize they were just a passing fancy."

Syril shook his head sharply. "I'm not a little child. I'm serious about becoming a warrior. Lord Scotus takes me seriously, even if no beast else does."

Skara's voice sharpened once more. "You seem to think this would be some grand, fun adventure. You have no idea what it means to be a real warrior."

"Then I could learn!" Syril pleaded. "Blackwell doesn't even have a champion right now and, I'm nearly as old as Maximus was when he fought Teivel. All I need is some beast to teach me and, I'll bet Lord Scotus would be willing to do it if no beast else will!"

Skara grimaced. "Yes, I'm sure he would. He's certainly encouraged you in this direction enough already." The recorder mouse contemplated the situation before him. "Syril," he said at last, "do you want to continue helping us read through the histories?"

Syril shuffled his sandals against the rampart stonework. "No."

Skara nodded. "I thought before it was just the bad weather and the gloomy confines of the archives that were distracting you, but I see now that your heart is not in this endeavor, even out here in the bright summer sun. Very well ... you are excused from this task. Go tell Neo that you will be able to help her with the bellringing duties from now on."

Syril stood and forlornly headed for the nearest flight of wall stairs. There was no pride to be had in dismissal from such an important Abbey project, especially when Skara had specifically requested him for the job.

Serius wordlessly looked after his older brother, utterly mystified as to Syril's present mood or why he wouldn't want to continue to help with their reading.

Grauparus leaned over and whispered something in Skara's ear. The historian straightened and called out, "Oh, and Syril?"

The departing novice paused at the top of the stairs.

"Personally, I think this whole business of wanting to become a warrior is silliness of the highest order," Skara said. "But, if you're really serious about it, Grauparus here will put in a good word for you with Graupuss, and we'll see what he has to say about it. If you can convince him that training you would be worth his while ... well, then it's up to him. I warn you, he won't be an easy taskmaster, although I daresay you'd rather train under him than Lord Scotus!"

Syril tried to hide his smile, but couldn't quite succeed. He took the wall steps two at a time, doing his best impersonation of a squirrel in his haste to seek out Blackwell's newly-appointed otter Skipper, and somehow managed to reach the lawns without breaking his neck.

Skara chuckled, shaking his head. "Ah, to be young and foolish again!"

"Yeah, ain't it grand?"Grauparus stood, excusing himself. "Lemme go get that mousie squared away wi' our Skip. Be back in a two shakes of me rudder!"

The young otter caught up to Syril halfway across the lawns. "Whoa, slow down there, Syril matey! Don'tcha want me there t' help make yer case t' Skip Graupuss fer ya?"

Syril stopped and turned to face Grauparus. "How come you talk like an otter some-times, and like a normal beast other times?"

Grauparus put a flipper to his breast in feigned offence. "You sayin' us otters ain't normal beasts?"

"You know what I mean," Syril laughed. "I've seen you in Brother Skara's classes speaking as properly as any mouse of the order."

Grauparus shrugged. "All me ... er, my ... otter mates talk the way they talk, and it just naturally rubs off on me. The little ones seem to like it when I speak that way, so I just sort of slip into it without thinking when I'm with younger beasts.

Syril regard the otter. Grauparus was just enough seasons older than Syril so that they'd never become close friends or playmates. They knew each other from some of the classes they'd shared and from seeing each other around the Abbey, but most of the time Grauparus was off with his fellow otters or his sparrow pal Pirphor while Syril and Serius kept to their mole friend Rufus and some of the younger children.

"I'm not a little kid, Brady."

"If I thought you were, then I wouldn't be taking you to see Skip, now would I?" He gave Syril a playful slap on the arm. "Listen, I dunno if you've got what it take t' be a warrior. But you seem pretty determined, an' that's half the battle right there. So might's well give it a try an' see what comes of it, eh?"

"Thanks. That's all I'm asking. If only every beast 'round here could see it that way. They all seem to think that just because I'm an orphan, and don't have any parents to impress that I'll be content to be a novice bellringer for the rest of my life."

"Well, I can sorta identify, bein' a half-orphan myself. My Mum died right after I was born, y'know."

"Yeah, I know. That's too bad. Serius and I were dropped off here as infants. Our parents probably still live somewhere out on the Western Plains. They just couldn't provide for us the way they wanted, so they left us to be raised at Blackwell."

"There's worse places to grow up, that's fer shore," Grauparus said. "My Dad Nantuma was just too much of a wanderin' spirit to ever settle down here. But with Skara and old Brother Rampor to school me, and Gorver and Neo to keep my rudder straight, and even the dear ol' Abbot and Abbess themselves to take an interest in my up-bringing, I had all the parenting a young beast could want. You can be sure you and Serius weren't stinted in that regard."

"No, I guess not. I'm not complaining, it's just that ... well, I feel I'm ready to become more than I am now, and I can't stand the idea of being kept from that, just because all the old beasts here think I'm still a child."

"Well said," Grauparus gave an encouraging nod. "So let's go see that Skipper of ours, and see about getting you that warrior's training you want!"

That night, Vondick took his turn as wall top sentry. And, as fate would have it, he was to have some company on the battlements.

Syril yawned, long and wide, then pawed at his eyes.

"A bit past your bed-time," Terious wryly observed.

"Oh, excuse me, Vondick, sir," Syril apologized, splashing some cold water onto his face from a nearby basin.

"If you're getting sleepy, Syril, you can go down whenever you want. You don't have to stay up here all night, you know."

These words brought the young mouse more fully awake than the water dripping from his whiskers. "Yes, I do, sir. Gorver assigned me to stand guard with you. If I don't stick out the full shift, he won't want to train me at all."

"Ahh. Well, I'm not much of a night beast myself, so I do appreciate the company to help keep me awake. Bit of a dirty trick, if you ask me, Graupuss setting a task for you that you're ill-equipped to manage. On the other paw, a real warrior will sometimes have to go without sleep while the creatures he protects are slumbering and, in time of war, keeping a vigilant watch can be as vital a part of the warrior's job as any swordplay. Perhaps this is a good first trial for you after all."

"Oh." When Syril had gone to Gorver that afternoon asking to be trained as a warrior, the otter Skipper had smiled and seemed highly amused by the whole thing. His assignment for Syril to stand watch tonight with Vondick had been tossed out like a dismissal, just to get the young mouse out of his fur. But now Vondick's words made Syril look at things anew. He had assumed Terious was to be his nursemaid, the experienced Forest Patrol leader playing the part of babysitter. But this squirrel knew as much of the warrior's art as any beast at Blackwell. Syril suddenly realized what an honor it was to stand watch with Vondick.

"Vondick, sir? You seem to be taking me more seriously about this than, the others ... "

"It's halfway toward dawn. I think that shows a lot of dedication right there. When I was a young student in Brother Rampor's classes, and learned the story of Maximus, I came to accept that true warriors may emerge from the most unlikely of places. So, if you say you want to be a warrior, I'll certainly give you the benefit of the doubt. If you're really serious..."

"I am! I swear it!"

"Then let this night begin your training, and we'll soon see if you have the stuff that makes a real warrior." Terious raised a paw and pointed out over the wall top into the darkness, somewhere to the southwest of Blackwell. "Look out that way, Syril, and tell me what you see."

Syril peered out over the battlement stone, straining his eyes to scan the dark countryside. The quarter-moon provided very little in the way of light. It was all Syril could
do to make out the dark gray ribbon of the main road snaking away into the south
of Primley, the dense tree growth forming a darker shadow against the night itself.
Across the road from Blackwell, the flat enlargement of the plains rolled away to the
west like a still and silent ocean, a lighter shade of gray than the road, but just as
featureless in the dim moonlight.

Vondick pointed to a spot of scattered copses, on the edge of the Western Plains
where the trees grew in isolated clusters before yielding completely to the flat grass-
lands. Syril stared at it. "I don't see anything, Vondick, sir."

"Look harder. Into the darkness beneath the trees."

Syril tried again. This time, after several moments, he could discern a faint flickering
coming from between the tree trunks. At this distance, it was brighter than the plains
around the copse. "I see it! Some beast has lit a fire in that stand of trees."

"That's right," the squirrel master said. "Good job, Syril. Your eyesight is quite sharp."

"Not as sharp as yours, sir. How did you ever - "

Terious held up a paw. "I only saw it myself because I knew right where to look.
Woody, who had this watch last night, reported seeing signs of a campfire across the
road to the south. Whatever beast is camped there, this is their second night in the
same spot. Strange, that. I think tomorrow some of us should go take a look."

"Do you suppose they've been there longer than just the last two nights?"

"Impossible to say. It was raining buckets the two nights before that, so there
wouldn't have been any fire to see and, we haven't had a proper patrol out since Lord
Scotus arrival, so ... Syril! Look out!"

Terious darted forward and pulled Syril down onto all fours. Syril heard the piercing
cry and felt the wind of the tremendous wing flaps before he actually saw the giant
bird pass over him and, then it was gone, before he could see just what it was.

Two more shrieks cut through the night, then quiet calm returned to Blackwell
Abbey. He and Vondick raised themselves into a cautious crouch.

"What was that?"

Terious shook his head. "Owls are the only birds that fly at night, normally, but that didn't look like an owl to me. Too big to be a bat. Strange ... very strange."

He stood all the way up, scanning the night sky as he dusted off his tunic. "And I've never heard a noise like that from any bird. Sounded like a signal, almost. Probably woke up half the Abbey."

"It might've gotten me, if you hadn't seen it coming and pulled me down just in time ... "

"I'm not so sure it was after us," Vondick said. "It still could have grabbed either of us if it had wanted to. I got the impression that it was as surprised to see us standing up here as we were to see it. I think it may even have veered away at the last moment to avoid hitting us. Perhaps it's not a creature that's used to flying at night."

"It doesn't seem to be coming back. Do you suppose it could have been the same falcon that visited Lord Scotus before the storm?"

"Could be ... although I think that monster that just flew over us was even bigger than Scotus's falcon."

Down on the dark and empty grounds, the silence was broken by the opening of the door to the main Abbey. The dim flicker of the Great Hall torches spilled out onto the lawns for a few seconds, then the wedge of light vanished again as the emerging figure closed the door behind it. Even in the near-blackness, there was no mistaking the hulking armored form.

"Speak of the devil," Vondick muttered.

Scotus strode across the lawns, making straight for the west wall steps. Climbing they bought him up to the ramparts just a few paces from the two watchers.

He might have nodded to them - it was too dark to be sure - but uttered no sound as he went to the high wall top over the main gate.

The badger held something in one paw. A sudden wash of weak light revealed it to be a lantern, which he'd kept covered until gaining the gatetop. Lifting the lamp high above his head, he swung it to and fro, describing a moving arch of pale light against the black of night.

"Now what do you suppose - "Syril started to whisper, but was cut short by a shoosh from Vondick.

Another of the unearthly shrieks came out of the night, and the winged giant materialized from the darkness to settle roughly upon the battlements along side the badger.

"It is the falcon!" Syril said in an excited hush. He'd been down in the archives when Scotus had last conferred with the winged officer, and was sorry he'd missed it. Now he was very glad he'd taken this late watch with Vondick.

But Terious shook his head. "No ... that's not a falcon. A kite, I think, although it's hard to be sure in the lamp light. But it definitely is a good deal bigger than the falcon that visited us before. Even Lord Scotus is dwarfed standing next to it!"

"How many birds does he have working for him?" Syril wondered.

"A very good question," said Terious, for it was obvious that Dun Scotus was indeed conferring with this night visitor just as he had with the falcon before the storm. "But those cries it gave out must have been a signal, as I suspected, considering how quickly Dun Scotus came out to meet it."

More Blackwellers had started to emerge at last from the main Abbey, standing upon the lawns in the small pool of light coming through the open door. None ventured any farther, content to watch Dun Scotus's walltop conference from a distance in case the winged giant proved less friendly toward unarmed woodlanders than toward armored badgers.

Dun Scotus replaced the cover over his lantern. He and the bird became a pair of massive silhouettes against the starry sky. Moments later there was heard the flapping of tremendous wings as the larger of the two shadow-shapes lifted from the wall top and disappeared into the night.

Vondick stepped forward to meet the Badger Lord at the top of the wall stairs. "What was all that about, Lord?"

"Routine reports, nothing more," Dun Scotus calmly replied, causing the Vondick to raise his eyebrows. The squirrel chief's eyebrows rose even higher as Dun Scotus continued, "I wish another council with the Abbey leaders first thing in the morning."

"Oh? Yet, you're sure that bird carried no urgent news?" Vondick's tone held open disbelief.

"If it had been urgent," Dun Scotus said, "I would call the council right now and not wait until the morning." He started down the wall steps.

"If you say so. Oh, one other thing, My Lord."

Dun Scotus paused on the top step to hear Vondick's report.

"For the past two nights, there have been sightings of a camp fire burning on the other side of the road to the south of here. It should be investigated. Do you think we should send out a party right now since most of us seem to be awake, or wait until daylight?"

The badger warrior seemed to mull it over for a moment. "I would not worry about it," he said at last, and continued on his way down to the dark lawns.

"Not worry about it!" Terious muttered. "And this from the very same beast who was so concerned with our security that he put us up here in the middle of the night to stand watches?" He turned to stare out at the barely-visible campfire once more. "There's something odd going on here. Too odd for my liking ... "

A hare, a mole and a shrew sat around the fire.

The hare lounged with his back against a tree trunk, one leg crossed over the other, his over-sized paddle foot tapping out a rhythm in midair. He was entertaining himself and his companions with a boisterous melody on a set of tuned wood pipes. By over-blowing against the holes, he was able to give the pipes' mellow, flute like tone a rougher and lively edge. His tune had the rowdy feel of a sea shanty, and if it had words they almost certainly would not have been appropriate for children's ears. He finished off with an up-beat flourish and set aside his instrument. His camp mates refrained from applauding, but showed their appreciation in a low-key manner with smiles and nods.

"Burr hurr, et wuz a gudd 'un, Weegard."

"Woulda done a sea otter proud," the shrew agreed. "Play us another, Weegard."

"Whoa, lemme catch my breath first!" the hare laughed, basking in the accolades. "A chap isn't made of wind, wot?"

"Depends what beast ye're talkin' 'bout," said the shrew. "I have known some in the north what were nuthin' but."

"Then I'm jolly well glad I never made their acquaintance." Weegard clasped his paws behind his head and stretched out his long legs in front of him. "Although in my distinguished career as a roving player and master thespian, I've known - er, known - quite a number of beasts. Takes all types to make a proper bally audience, wot? Fer instance, I recall with no small fondness my engagement before the ruling court of Noonvale ... "

"Hurr, brudder, 'ere 'ee goes again," the mole muttered, rolling his tiny eyes.

"Yeah, no more o' yer rem'nisses about yer one night stands, Weegard, we heard 'em all already. We know you've 'ad t'play fer yer supper or go hungry, jus' like the rest o' us." The shrew snorted. "Master actor - ha!"

Weegard pulled a petulent lower lip. "Well, Dun Scotus seems to have a higher opinion of my acting abilities than you blokes, else he wouldn't have chosen me for this special duty."

"Yah, 'cos you were the only hare actor he could find." The shrew looked around, into the night beyond the firelight. "I'm startin' to wonder if'n we'll ever hear from that badger again."

"Oh, no doubt about that, Jarbo me old shrew. Besides, wot're you complainin' about? We've got a beautiful summer night an' all the world is ours to enjoy. Sure beasts that dank old log where we had to shelter two days straight during that dreadful storm. I thought we were going to float right away!"

"Yurr roight 'bout that, Weegard," said the mole. "Oi'm gurtly afeared o' water deeper'n moi 'ead. Most of uz molers are." He closed his eyes and lay down on a bed of moss. "Oi'll be takin' sum shutoi noaw. If'n you play anymore, Weegard, make et a noice quoiet 'un please, zurr."

"Righto, Somwand chappie. Just happens I know a nice little lullabye, the bally thing for serenading sleepin' babes and moles in the woods." The hare once more raised the pipes to his lips and blew out a soft, slow string of notes, a whispering melody gentle as the summer night breeze. Somwand sighed in molish contentment as he lay upon the moss, but Bobra clearly preferred a more spirited tune and quickly grew restless, fidgiting upon his log seat.

Sensing his shrew companion's mood, Weegard paused in his playing to cast Bobra a knowing glance over the top of the pipes. "By the by, this one also goes over great with th' gels."

Bobra grinned. "Yeah, right. You've had as many females as I've had dinners with the King of the Moon!"

"Hey, have a care with that talk, Jarbsy mate! Them's fightin' words to a hare!"

"Fightin' words, eh? Then, come have at me, you flop-eared fool. You know I kin lick yer any day, blindfolded an' wi' one paw tied behind my back."

Weegard's indignant pose instantly deflated. He might have been able to fool a stranger, but his companions knew he was no fighting beast. "Oh, life can be so hard for a simple traveling actor."

"Oh yeah?" Bobra countered. "Try fightin' in a battle sometime, an' you will see how hard life can be."

"An' sully my reputation as a peaceful ambassador of the arts? Never, sah!"

"Quioet, gennel beasts!" Somwand moaned. "Oi'm troin' t' sleep!"

"Sorry, chap." Weegard held a paw to his lips. "Some silence for the mole, Bobra," he whispered in mock seriousness.

"Don'tcha mean 'soilence?'" The hare and shrew chuckled softly together, and Weegard made to resume his lilting lullabye. Barely had he begun to blow his notes than the smooth song of the pipes was drowned out by the crashing of tree growth overhead and the rush of mighty flapping wings.

Somwand came instantly awake and alert, rolling away from the fire to hide behind a tree. Bobra joined him a moment later, but Weegard sat his ground, gazing nervously up at the kite that now dominated the camp clearing.

The immense bird of prey could probably have lifted all three of them at once with little effort. But this particular kite was known to them, and Weegard knew he was in no danger. Still, it was impossible not to be at least a little intimidated, being so close to such a mighty hunter of the sky.

"Hullo, Nelogan," Weegard said to the bird. "Been waitin' the bloody longest time for you to show. Glad you finally made it."

The kite - a female of majestic proportions - stared across the glade at the shrew and mole peeking out at her from behind their treetrunks, then turned her steely gaze upon the hare.

"Dun Scotus says you go now."

"Righto," Weegard gave a carefree salute. "First thing in the morning, I'm off."

Nelogan shook her great feathered head. "No, not morning. Now. This night."

Weegard sputtered in exasperation. "But ... but I haven't had a decent nights sleep goin' on four nights now, 'cos I've been stayin up waitin' for you."

"Yeah," Bobra whispered to Somwand from behind his tree, "he's been gettin' all his sleep during the day, an' we're the ones who've had to listen to his snorin'!"

"Hurr hurr hurr."

Weegard went on, "I need to rest up before I can embark on such a bally sprint."

"Your problem. Dun Scotus says leave tonight. Your fire was seen from Blackwell. They could have come to investigate."

"Oh, and wot would they have found? Just a jolly little trio of harmless woodlanders camped out for the night, enjoyin' each other's humble company. No harm done."

Nelogan blinked in the firelight, immune to any argument from the hare. "You leave tonight," she said curtly, then took flight without another word. The wind from her wings fanned the fire, scattering embers and ash all around the small clearing. Weegard had to wave his paws in front of his face to keep the dancing red sparks from going into his eyes.

"Well, I never ... " Weegard looked toward Bobra and Somwand, emerging from behind their shelter. "How's a chaps suppose to undertake a journey like this on such blinkin' short notice? Why, I'm tempted to bed down right here through to morning, just to show that cold featherbag!"

"Uh, I wouldn't, if'n I was you," Bobra said. "If Lord Scotus wants you to get started tonight, you'd best do just that."

"Ee's roight, Weegard," Somwand agreed. "You'm doant be wantin' that moighty stroipedog mad at you, no zurr."

Weegard pursed his lips. "You chaps're probably right. Ah, well, no rest for the wicked, I suppose." The hare cast about him, gathering up this and strapping on that, and in no time at all he was travel-ready. Everything he would need for this trip was tucked into the pouches and compartments of his travel belts, and a haversack of extra food and drink was slung across his back. He carried no weapons; this was a mission for speed, and Weegard was sure he could out run any beast who might try to pick a fight. When it came to confrontation, Weegard's specialty was flight.

He paused when he came to his musical pipes, wondering whether he should try to squeeze them into the haversack with the extra food. At length he turned to Somwand and held the instrument out to the mole.

"No time for music where I'm going, I'm 'fraid. Keep these safe for me, Somwand ol' pal, an' I'll collect 'em from you when we meet again."

"Hurr, you'm shure 'bout this, Weegard? They'm yurr faveritt possesshurn."

"That's why I'm trustin''em to a nice sensible chappie like you. Moles're proper respectable beasts about carin' for things." Weegard shook paws with Bobra and Somwand.

"Yurr ... take care, Weegard, burr hurr."

"Watch out fer yerself," Bobra said. "An' break a leg."

"Not while I'm going over those bally mountains, I hope. See you both later this season, if all goes well and I jolly well hope it does." Weegard hefted the sack and walked off into the darkness of the trees beyond the firelight, calling back over his shoulder, "I'm off to Astapailia!"

CHAPTER 9

Learning that Lord Scotus wanted to hold another council of the Abbey elders to coincide with breakfast, Friar Calgarus spread the big table in the Great Hall with a lavish variety of food and drink. When Brae and the others came down for the start of the meeting, they were greeted by a display of cinnamon toast with butter, quince tarts, and a deluxe apple and spice cake topped with sweet crushed hazelnut crumbs. Drinks included honeyed milk, cool mint tea and grape and cherry cordials. Graupuss was, naturally, the first to tuck into the delectable-looking cake, forcing a hefty wedge onto his plate between slices of toast and warm tarts. The others helped themselves to more modest portions, and filled their cups with their beverages of choice. Dun Scotus satisfied himself with two pieces of toast and a tumbler of cool water.

The Badger Lord waited until all present had finished serving themselves, so that he could speak without distractions. This gathering was the same as the first council on the afternoon of his arrival, with one exception: the Abbess had decided it was too early to summon Strongwing, so the Celtar leader was absent from this session.

But the rest of the Abbey leaders - Brae, Graupulous, Skara, Gorver, Vondick, Neo and Hollnow - were with Dun Scotus at the table.

Friar Calgarus and his staff withdrew up the stairs to the Great Hall so that the eight of them could have the Great Hall all to themselves. Unless some emergency arose up above, no beast would intrude until the Abbess emerged to declare the council concluded.

Like a hungry force of nature, Graupuss reached for his second slice of cake while most of the others were just getting started on their first helpings. Recognizing that they would be here all day if he waited for the otter Skipper to stop eating, Dun Scotus began.

"I concluded our last meeting by saying that there was much more to be told, of my prophecy and my activities to prepare for it. Now that improvements in Blackwell's defenses are under way and I have given you the full measure of my warrior's counsel, the time has come to speak of these things."

Every Blackweller at the table, even Graupuss, gave Dun Scotus their undivided attention. So far, the badger warrior had deflected all their inquiries about the bird which had visited the night before, refusing to discuss the matter until the council was under way. They were almost eager to hear his explanation of that event.

What he was to tell them that morning, however, would make them forget all about the night visitor.

"I have told you that my prophecy foretells a great crisis, which I believe may be nearly upon us. I have also told you that the prophecy is vague about the exact nature of this crisis, or the direction from which it will come. There may be war, or perhaps a series of wars, on a scale unprecedented in all the history of the lands. Twenty seasons ago, when fate first spoke through me and my paw carved this doom into the living rock of Astapailia, I bent the entirety of my mind and will toward a possible solution to this threat. I asked myself, over and over, what action might I take to best meet this coming upheaval? At last I decided upon a course that I felt was the only way to prepare for these difficult times.

"Since the prophecy does not reveal which creatures will involve themselves in the fighting, I reasoned that any beast could turn out to be our enemy ... or our ally. The lands are full of vermin and foxes and other species who are the traditional bane of decent creatures. If the threat to peace is to come from without, from Jurista and his searats or some dark kingdom as yet unknown to us, then the vermin of Primley and the Northlands will no doubt ally themselves with the invaders and fight against the good beasts of the lands.

Then again, perhaps the threat is to come from within our own territories. Warlords have emerged from less likely places than your own Primley Woods, and a chieftain who could unite all rats, foxes, weasels, stoats and ferrets - and teach them how to wage real war - would prove as deadly to us as any searat king or invading army from parts unknown. In either case, it is clear that the vermin living among us are a danger and a threat, and one that must be eliminated."

And with that, Dun Scotus reached for his tumbler of water and helped himself to a long draught of it.

It was easy to draw the obvious conclusion from the badger's words. Most of the Blackwellers were so shocked by what Dun Scotus seemed to be suggesting that Abbess Brae took it upon herself to address the issue before he could continue.

"My Lord, if your plan is to slaughter all the vermin and foxes of Primley, then we must oppose you. Such a tactic might be acceptable in the Northlands, but we could not sit idly by and allow such a thing to take place in Primley, much less be a part of it. If this is what you're suggesting..."

Dun Scotus raised a paw to stop her. "You misunderstand me. It is true that I have slain many beasts in the north, but only those who proved themselves my enemy by word or deed. I could never kill all the vermin of the lands, even if I were to labor at such a task for another twenty seasons, and another twenty after that." He shook his head. "No, what I am attempting is far more ambitious than such a slaughter ... although you may question it nearly as much."

The Blackwellers didn't know what to make of this. "Go on," Brae said.

"There is a saying in the north that an enemy kept close at paw is less dangerous than one held at a distance. My plan, quite simply, is to keep our potential enemies so close that they are given no chance to become our enemies. An invading warlord would not be able to use our weasels, rats and foxes as weapons against us, if we have already forged them into a weapon of our own."

Old Abbot Graupulous adjusted the spectacles on the end of his nose.

"Are you saying, Lord, that you mean to take some of these creatures into your service, and put them under arms?"

"Not some. All."

"Impossible!" Vondick cried out, displaying more of the agitation he'd shown the day before over the tree-cutting proposal.

"It has already begun," said Dun Scotus. "In the north, I have laid down my gauntlet far and wide to every rat, fox, weasel, ferret and stoat in those lands: join my cause for the benefit of all creatures, or remain my enemy and be slain. You would be amazed to learn how many have already chosen my service over continued struggle and death."

Brae said to Dun Scotus, "Not having seen it with my own eyes, I must say I share Vondick's skepticism. What you describe is difficult for us to imagine. Please tell us more about how you have done this."

"Certainly. I believe nearly every creature is born with a noble spirit, and evil ways must be learned. Only a very few become truly evil beyond all redemption. If those few are eliminated and their influence wiped clean from the face of the lands, then most of their followers can be made to serve the cause of good rather than evil. Most vermin are misguided and lacking in a decent upbringing and, since honest creatures tend to shun and distrust them, they are given no chance to prove their decency.

Their noble spirit is given no freedom to flower. Inevitably they band together with others of their own kind, and that is where they learn savage ways and selfishness, with the truly evil ones emerging as horde leaders, captains, tyrants and warlords since they will put down and murder even their fellow vermin to gain power.

"This is how it has been for more generations than any beast can remember and, it has led to great suffering and constant war. But with the coming crisis, these old ways must be abandoned if we hope to survive. All creatures must learn to trust one another, to live peacefully side by side. This I, truly believe is our best hope to weather the coming storm, and perhaps even prevent it and, all my efforts these past twenty seasons have been aimed toward achieving this goal.

"As to how I have been going about this, it has proven simpler than you might suppose. Every time word reaches me of a horde terrorizing good beasts, I assemble my forces and march to meet it in battle. So far, I have never lost. Once the horde leaders are slain, along with any other of their numbers I judge to be treacherous or dangerous, I offer their surviving followers the choice to join my army, or lay down their arms to never again trouble decent creatures, upon pain of death. As you may imagine, I have not had to face many of them on the battlefield a second time and, most do join me, rather than try to fend for themselves in the wild, leaderless and subject to the ill will of good beasts they'd formerly terrorized."

"I don't see how you can control them all," commented Brae. "If you truly have armed them and trained them well, aren't you concerned that some of the nastier ones might try to kill you and take command of your army as their own horde?"

"There were several attempts to do just that in the early days of my campaigns. Every beast who tried is dead now, while I am still very much alive."

This simple statement in fact sent chills down the spines of several of the Blackwellers.

"It has been several seasons since any would-be tyrant from within my own ranks has challenged me. But most of my soldiers are decent creatures who would never accept the leadership of such a beast. The many shrews, otters, squirrels and mice under my command ensure that no evil-minded vermin would ever be able to take over my forces, even if they should succeed in killing me."

"All those woodland creatures?" Brae said in surprise. "Do they march alongside vermin and foxes?"

"That is the entire point of my enterprise," said Dun Scotus. "We have all put aside past differences for the greater good of all. My troops no longer look upon each other as rats or mice, otters or foxes, shrews or weasels. They are all fighters working toward a common goal, each judged solely according to its ability, and each given the same respect that any creature would want for itself."

Quiet fell over the Great Hall. No revelation of Dun Scotus's could have aroused a greater mix of conflicted feeling among the Blackwellers. Their order had been founded on the very principle that Dun Scotus had just spoken. Blackwell was a haven and sanctuary for all beasts in need, no matter their species. Even Teivel the Terrible had been extended the Abbey's hospitality, until he showed his hostile intentions. On the other paw, they'd suffered so much loss from these creatures throughout their history that they'd come to regard all vermin as enemies.

The idea that Dun Scotus had taken so many of these beasts into his service and placed them under arms was an unsettling one to them, regardless of the Badger Lord's assurances.

Brother Skara had been rendered speechless by all of this. Finding his voice at last, he said, "I still cannot believe how this could possibly work. Tell us, just how successful you have been in controlling your vermin, and how the other Northlanders feel about what you are doing."

"Things in the north have always been pretty much the same as here," Dun Scotus explained. "That is to say, there are the decent, honest creatures, many of whom farm for a living, and then there are the thieves and barbarians who produce nothing for themselves and must take what they need from others or else starve. I took a long look at this state of affairs, and realized that if the farmers and growers of food did not have to expend so much effort fighting off those who would steal it, they could produce much more ... enough to feed the very foes who would otherwise take it by force and, harvests have indeed improved in the regions where I have been at work, with many formerly barren acres now transformed into fertile and productive croplands. The vermin who in the past would have raided these farms now march under my banner to protect those very harvests. It is a new way, and one that benefits everybeast. The honest creatures no longer live in fear of losing everything to a raiding horde, and the vermin no longer go hungry. A beast who knows where its next meal is coming from is much less likely to cause trouble and, I do keep my troops well-fed."

"Sounds like a paradise," Skara said skeptically, then shrank in his seat at the narrow-eyed gaze the badger warrior trained upon him.

"Hardly. The lands are still harsh, and many foebeasts remain outside my control and, there are good-hearted creatures who have known the old ways for so long that they will always be suspicious of their former enemies. But by creating this standing army, I have not only forged a potent weapon to meet the coming crisis, but also found a solution to the ages-old history of conflict between vermin and honest creatures. It is a fundamental change in the way things have always been, and something that should have been attempted long before now. So much sufferng could have been prevented."

It was then that Gorver asked a question which had not occurred to any of his fellow Blackwellers.

"I say, M'Lord, how does yer brother feel 'bout all this? Can't imagine too many badgers-in-arms wantin' to cozy up to rats 'n' weasels. Or his fightin' hares wantin' to march alongside 'em."

"He has not involved himself in my campaigns," Dun Scotus replied coolly.

"And why would that be?" the Abbess pressed, when it became clear Dun Scotus did not intend to elaborate further.

"My brother Nantrom has all he can do to hold Astapailia and the coastlands against King Jurista and the searats. I have followed my own path for the sake of the salvation of the lands, and he has followed his. One of us had to remain at Astapailia, obviously. By holding the coastlands secure, he has allowed me the freedom to pursue what I feel is the best hope for all creatures. His work has been no less vital than my own. I have not visited my mountain home in many seasons. I am hoping to journey there once I leave Blackwell, if circumstances allow."

The tone of impassioned authority and finality in his tone was such that not one of the Blackwellers noticed Dun Scotus had not answered Graupuss's question at all.

"I still say this is a dangerous thing you are doing," Skara insisted. "As Blackwell's historian, I am very well versed in the ways our Abbey has suffered at the paws of power-hungry vermin over the seasons. It seems to me that you could be creating a terrible engine of destruction, which might prove unstoppable if it should ever turn against us."

"If you know how the lands have suffered under the old ways," the Badger Lord calmly responded, "then you more than anybeast should see the truth of all I have said here."

"Well, yes, but ... if the force of your will proves insufficient to keep your war machine under control... "

"Ahh ... But you should not underestimate the force of my will. It has already allowed me to tame much of the Northlands and slay many of the worst horde leaders.

A prophecy of doom was laid upon me twenty seasons ago, when I was touched by the paw of fate. This has never left me. The force of my will have the power of destiny behind it." Dun Scotus drew his sword and laid it upon the table amidst the breakfast items. It was the first time any of the Blackwellers had glimpsed the blade up close; the mighty weapon was dull with age and use, except along its double cutting edges, which shone with a keen sharpness where they weren't notched or pitted. While not as splendid as the majestic sword of Septimus, it was every bit as much the blade of a true warrior.

"The evil beasts of the north have come to know this weapon well, and those who still survive fear it. But its power goes beyond killing. This blade has also made enemies into allies, and brought peace of mind to terrorized good beasts.
No enemy has been able to best me since I began my Northlands campaigns, and it is my intention that none ever shall. My actions are to create peace, not destroy it." Dun Scotus addressed the entire council. "I have told you all of this for several reasons. First, you are entitled to an explanation of what I have been doing in the Northlands, and why. I had promised you this, and now I have fulfilled that promise.
"More important was the fact that you heard this from me rather than some beast else. I have made enemies in my campaigns, many of whom realize they would stand no chance against me on the battlefield. These foes must resort to another weapon instead: lies. Since my aims could be easily misunderstood, my enemies often try to divide the honest creatures with falsehoods about what I am trying to do, creating distrust among the allies I must have to complete my work. If they had somehow managed to tell you that I have taken vermin and foxes into my ranks before I'd had the opportunity to properly explain myself, then they might have succeeded in sowing doubts and suspicions among you. I took a chance waiting as long as I did, but I wanted to address the defenses of this Abbey before all else and, what I have told you this morning could only have been said at a full council, as I am sure you all understand."
"Yes, I can see why," Brae concurred. "But I have a question. You have told us that some of your forces are right here in Primley. I take it there are vermin among them?"
"Naturally. When I was getting ready to journey south, I chose to accompany me those troops whose skills would be of greatest benefit. They were selected for their abilites as individuals, not their species."
"Still," said Graupulous, "it was chancy bringing such a force to our lands, where creatures like that are held in suspicion and distrust."
"There has been no trouble so far," Dun Scotus said. "But that is another reason I wanted to inform you of all this. Someday you may see a group of creatures traveling these lands, and that group might include rats or foxes, stoats or ferrets, or may even be headed by such a beast. You can no longer assume that they are enemies because they might be mine."
"How will we be able to tell?" asked the Abbess.

"For the near future, I will be here to let you know which creatures are in my service. But even after I leave Blackwell, you will know. My soldiers carry themselves with a dignity that no thief or villain would be able to imitate and, if you see woodlanders such as otters, mice and shrews marching with them, you will know them to be friends."

Gorver gave Vondick a knowing nudge with his elbow. "Can't say I've ever seen a rat or weasel wot was dignified. Hafta see it to believe it."

"No," agreed Terious, "although a fox could probably put on a good show of it. Those crafty beasts can fool a woodlander into believing anything."

Dun Scotus turned to the otter and squirrel. "You are not the first good beasts to show such doubts and, if you should someday chance to meet any of my troops, I am sure you will also not be the first to be pleasantly surprised, so long as you keep an open mind."

"Can we expect to see them here at Blackwell any time soon?" asked the Abbess. "You said you'd give us some notice, so we can prepare to receive them."

"My forces move as the situation dictates," Dun Scotus replied. "We shall see what the days ahead bring."

"As long as your band is so close, they might as well visit Blackwell," old Graupulous suggested. "After all, they've come so far and, it would give us a chance to see for ourselves your noble and honest vermin."

"Although" added Brae, "you would have to promise that they would cause no harm if we let them into our Abbey."

"Of course. I am here to aid and assist Blackwell. I would never permit anything that would harm good beasts, or disrupt their way of life."

"Bit too late for that last part," Vondick whispered to Gorver from the corner of his mouth.

Brae, Graupulous and Hollnow remained at the table with Lord Scotus after the others had left to resume their regular duties. They wanted to discuss the proposed Great Hall stairs.

"Facts be facts, gennelmoice," Hollnow said to the Abbess and retired Abbot. " Thurr doan't be enuff stone 'n' wood at our Habbey t' carnstruct ee starway so hoigh. Uz'll need t' reopern ee quarry."

"That's more work than we bargained for," Brae said. "The quarry is a good half day's march to the east, on the other side of the River Primley. We'll need shrew boats to ferry tools and workers across, and to bring back the cut stone. Building these stairs could take us until next winter, or even spring!"

"There should be no problem cutting the necessary stone and timber and getting it all to Blackwell before the start of the cold winter weather," Dun Scotus rumbled. " My blueprints are most precise. We will know to the exact brick and beam what will be required, and in what sizes. Once all the material is on paw, construction can commence at its own speed. Since all the work from that point on will take place indoors, it can be done even in the chill depths of winter."

"Still, it will be a greater task than we envisioned," Graupulous nodded.

"But it might well be worth the ... " Brae let her voice trail off in midsentence as the faint sound of the Maximus and Neltron bells came down into the Great Hall. She cocked her head and listened for a moment. "Oh, no not another storm!"

Graupulous listened along with her. "I think that's what it's supposed to be, but Neo's making the same mistake as last time, so it sounds more like the call to arms. Funny ... with the training she's had with Syril and Serius, I'd have thought she'd be able to get it right this time."

"Well, I'd best go see what it's all about," said the Abbess. "I hope it's a false alarm. The last thing our poor beleaguered gardens need is another storm! If you will excuse me, My Lord."

Brae went up the stairs into the Great Hall and was on her way to go outside when the squirrel Woody appeared in the doorway in front of her. He stopped with one paw on the jamb, breathing hard as if he'd just run down from the wall steps.

"Abbess ... there you are! I was just ... coming to get you," he panted.

"Storm coming, Woody?" Brae asked, lifting a paw to indicate the bells.

Woody shook his head. "Army coming ... down the road. Huge one. Vermin ... must be hundreds of 'em and, they're armed for battle!"

Brae's eyebrows shot up. Could it possibly be? No, Dun Scotus had indicated his presence here in Primley was a small detachment of his main forces. "Are you sure it's not just a score or two?"

"Oh no, Abbess ma'am. I was up on the wall ... I saw 'em myself. It's like Teivel's army reborn, and marching straight toward us. Hundreds at least ... maybe a thousand."

"All vermin? Or are there any woodlanders marching with them?"

"Huh?" The question made no sense to Woody, who had not yet been apprised of the morning council. "Uh, why would there be?"

Brae glanced back over her shoulder toward the Great Hall, where Dun Scotus still tarried with Hollnow and Graupulous. Should she go inform them? No, first things first. She looked at Woody again. "I guess I'd better get out there to see this for myself."

The ramparts atop the west wall were crowded with Blackwellers, alerted to the approaching horde by the squirrel lookouts and Neo's mighty bellringing efforts. The squirrels had been the first to spot the giant dust cloud from the road, rising above the forest canopy to the north. Two hot summer days since the storm had dried the main path enough so that any large group of marchers would raise plumes of dust to mark their passage and, by the look of the roiling brown-white cloud hovering over the treetops, this army must be huge.

Woody had stuck around long enough for the actual marchers to become visible in the distance. Seeing that, they were indeed vermin carrying weapons of war, he'd raced down the wallstairs to fetch the Abbess and Vondick and Gorver and any beast else of authority he could find. Neo, out with the children on the lawns, heard his report and ran to sound the bells. Now the badger matriarch met Brae and Woody at the foot of the wall stairs, following them up to the wall-top.

"Graupuss and his otters are checking all the wall gates to make sure they're securely bolted and locked," Neo informed them, breathing hard from her climb up and down the bell tower. "If this horde means to make trouble, they will have a tough time getting into Blackwell."

"Let's hope they didn't bring a battering ram," Woody worried.

"No problem if they did," Vondick announced from above, striding along the wall-top to greet them at the top of the steps with longbow in paw. "I was just getting ready to take out a patrol when I heard the bells and all the shouting. We've got bows strung and quivers packed, enough to pick off scores of vermin if they try anything like that." He glanced out at the approaching army. "If they are vermin," he muttered under his breath.

112

Woody took his place at the battlements, reading his own bow. "So long as they don't have archers of their own, shooting back at us, sir."

"Maybe I should get some cauldrons from the kitchens," Neo suggested, "and start boiling some oil up here in case we need it to pour on them."

"Neo!" Brae declared, surprised that her badger friend could even entertain such a blood thirsty notion. "We don't even know if these beasts are our enemies yet. Let's save that kind of talk until we find out who they are."

"They sure aren't friends, from what I saw," said Woody.

Neo and Brae stepped up to the battlements themselves, and immediately saw both the dust cloud telltales above the trees, and the creatures who were kicking it up. Brae gasped in spite of herself; not even Woody's description had prepared her for the sight of so many beasts marching in brisk military formation.

The low thundering of so many stamping footpaws could be faintly heard from here, although the leading edge of the horde was still too distant to make out individual beasts in the shimmering air of summer morning.

Neo looked to the keen-eyed squirrels, who were raptly scanning the immense troop column. "What can you see? Are they all vermin, or are there any woodland creatures among them?"

The badger's question mystified most of the squirrels, but Vondick knew what she was getting at. "You mean, what Dun Scotus told us about this morning? But this can't be them ... there are too many!"

"That's what I was thinking myself," said Brae. "But we have to be sure. What do you see?"

Terious squinted his eyes as he peered into the distance. "Hard to tell yet. This far away, otters can look like weasels and squirrels can look like foxes, even to us. That dust they're putting up isn't any help. But I'll wager my bushtail that those are foxes I see marching ahead of the rest ..." He strained harder, shading his eyes with one paw, "... backed up by weasels, ferrets and stoats."

"All vermin," Neo said somberly.

Little Rufus the hedgehog had led a few of his young playmates up to the ramparts at the sound of the bells, hoping to see another monster storm looming on the horizon. What he saw now suited him even better. "Lookit that horde!" he exclaimed with glee. "Must be the hugest army ever t' pass through Primley!"

"Uh, Neo," Brae motioned to the badger, "please take these young ones down from here. I don't want them in harm's way, in case there's any trouble."

"But Motha' Abbess!" Rufus protested. "We wanna see th' army!"

"You've seen all you need to," Neo said in her no-nonsense manner. "Down we go now … follow me!" Fortunately, Rufus's friends were less enchanted and more fearful at the sight of the horde, and were more than happy to follow Neo and Rufus down onto the lawns.

Vondick gazed at the approaching army in consternation. "Those can't be Lord Scotus's troops. There are just too many! and, all of them vermin."

"Well, there's one beast who can answer this question for us. If those are his troops, I want Dun Scotus up here to tell us, and to explain what so many are doing in Primley and, if they're not, I still want him here to help us organize our defenses against this horde. That's what he keeps telling us he is coming to Blackwell for … so some beast please go get him! He's down in the Great Hall with Hollnow."

Woody jumped to do his Abbess's bidding, racing down the wall steps once more.

All around them, Blackwellers who still hadn't heard about Dun Scotus having vermin in his service were naturally assuming that the Abbey was under attack.

"Look at that horde! We could never stand against them!"

"They'll lay siege to the Abbey, and batter down the gates!"

"What should we do?"

"We'll be over run, shore 'nuff."

A clanging of steel against stone instantly silenced the panicked Abbey dwellers, and every beast turned to see Gorver standing on the top step of the wall stairs, the sword of Septimus in his paw.

"Let's not be hasty, folks! Perhaps these ain't our enemies. But if'n they are, we'll give 'em th' same kinda fight Blackwell's given every blusterin' brute who's ever crossed us, and send their survivors runnin' with tails 'tween their legs. This here's Blackwell, an' no foebeast will lay claim to it while I'm Skipper of otters!"

Ularus the hedgehog cellar keeper voiced the question shared by many of the other Blackwellers around her. "Huh? Whattaya mean, they may not be enemies? They're vermin, an' they're armed fer war. No horde like that 'un has ever passed us by without tryin' t' take Blackwell for their own."

"This time could be different," Brae told Ularus. "I hope." She glanced down and saw Dun Scotus striding across the Abbey lawns behind Woody toward the west wall steps. "Ah, there he is. Maybe now we can get some answers, and find out whether we are facing friend or foe."

The badger warrior climbed the stairs and joined them on the wall top, showing no more emotion than he ever did. "My Lord," Brae said to him, "we seem to be under attack, but we can't be sure after what you told us earlier. Please," she pointed out over the battlements at the approaching army, "tells us what this means to you."

To every beast's surprise, Dun Scotus reached down and detached a small metal tube from the side of his armor. Brae had assumed it was some mere decoration, but now saw that it was a separate device of the same red steel as his armor, held in place by a spring clamp.

Their puzzlement grew when he pulled at it, and the tube suddenly became twice as long as before. Dun Scotus twisted off metal caps from either end of the instrument, revealing the sparkle of highly polished glass lenses. Holding the tube up to one eye, the badger sighted through it at the approaching warbeasts.

Brae didn't want to disturb Dun Scotus, who seemed wholly concentrated on whatever it was that he was doing. "Uh ... My Lord ... "

Dun Scotus lowered the tube and called out in a booming voice, "Open the gate!" The Blackwellers were too startled to move right away; many thought their badger guest had gone mad. "Open the gates, Lord?" Woody asked, confused.

Dun Scotus gestured toward the distant army with his metal tube. "They carry the standard of the Badger War Lord. This is my army."

CHAPTER 10

For many moments the Blackwellers on the ramparts around Dun Scotus merely stared at him, especially those who had not been privy to the mornings council; more than one jaw hung agape in disbelief. Some turned to look anew over the wall at the nearing army, seeing it now in a different light, but no less awed by its size. In the hazy summer distance the masses of ranked marchers filled the dry road like a giant rippling snake winding its way down a narrow muddy stream, its width spanning from bank to bank. The midmorning sun glinted from a sea of shields, spears, swords and other instruments of war. It was the largest army that Blackwell had seen since the horde of Teivel the Terrible.

Brae said to Dun Scotus, her tone quite severe, "You told us you would give us some notice before any large number of your forces came to Blackwell, so we would have time to properly prepare for them."

"I also told you," Dun Scotus answered unapologetically, "that I would try to arrange a demonstration to prove to you that a large horde could come upon Blackwell without warning. My troops force-marched through the night to provide this. Later I will discuss with you when we may commence cutting down the trees outside the wall, now that I have proven my point. But first I must go out and greet my captains. Please have the gate opened, Abbess."

Brae made no move to comply. "No trees will be fall until we have given that matter a great deal more thought and discussion." She could see Vondick standing behind Dun Scotus, and had spoken as much to the squirrel as to the badger. "More to the point, when you told us at the meeting this morning that you had some vermin in your service, you gave no indication that nearly all your soldiers were such beasts. I see no woodlanders in that horde out there."

"You are not looking closely enough," Dun Scotus said matter-of-factly. "Some of the marchers you mistake for stoats, ferrets and weasels at this distance are actually otters; I have many of those in my service and, there is a squirrel in the front ranks with the foxes. Farther back in the column, as you will shortly see, are squads of hedgehogs, shrews and mice. They are hidden by the taller creatures in front of them." He held out his metal tube. "Here. See for yourself."

Vondick reached around Dun Scotus and grabbed the tube before the Abbess could take it. Turning it over in his paws, he asked, "Ur ... what does this do?"

"I call it a long glass. It makes things far away look closer. Point the wide end at the army, and gaze through the narrow lens with one eye, as I just did."

Terious was skeptical, but did as told. When he finally had it sighted properly and gazed through the device, he gave a start and stepped backward, almost throwing himself off the high wall onto the Abbey lawns below.

"Gads!" Steadying himself, Vondick gave the tube in his paws an incredulous, amazed stare. "It's like they're right in front of me." Going back to the outer edge of the ramparts, he gave a second, longer peer through the instrument. "Oh, yes, I can see the otters now ... and the squirrel, a female ... can't see any smaller beasts, the rear of the column is hidden by too much dust. By the fur that army is huge!" The squirrel chief passed the long glass to Brae for the Abbess to have a look for herself, then turned to the Badger Lord. "You led us to believe that only a small part of your forces came with you to Primley."

"That is correct. For every soldier you see on that road, I have a score more back in the Northlands."

Terious gaped. "But ... that would be thousands and thousands!"

Dun Scotus merely nodded. "The Northlands are a big place."

Brae lowered the long glass, passing it along to Gorver, who was eagerly awaiting his own turn to peer through it. "From what I see, Lord, the vermin out there still out number woodlanders by quite a bit. Will it be safe to have so many coming to Blackwell?"

"I will vouch for their good behavior, Abbess. They will know better than to cause you any trouble."

Still Brae gave no order to have the gate opened. "My Lord, we have taken you at your word in everything you have told us since coming here. But the safety of this Abbey and its creatures is my responsibility. I will not admit so many vermin into Blackwell until I am quite satisfied for myself that they will pose no danger."

"I understand. I can review the troops just as easily out in the road. You may join me if you wish."

"We both will," Vondick said, placing a protective paw on Brae's shoulder.

"Us, too," added Gorver, speaking for his otters.

"Obviously," Dun Scotus went on, "there are not enough rooms or beds in the Abbey for any, but a small few of my forces. I'd intended that they could camp out on your lawns, but if you cannot bring yourselves to allow certain creatures within these walls, I can station them in the field outside the south wall."

"We'll see," Brae said.

For the next few minutes they all stood in silence upon the walltop, watching as the mighty army drew up before Blackwell. A score of foxes, garbed in black tunics and wearing broadswords, headed the column, along with a strong-looking female squirrel who carried a full quiver of arrows and a majestic yew longbow.

The lead fox jumped forward as the column came to the gate, turning himself to face the marchers.

Drawing his sword and raising it high, he called out the order to halt. The massive procession came to a staggered, shuffling stop as the order made its way back through the ranks. Under the bright morning sun, all the dust that their paws had kicked up now began to settle backdown upon the hundreds of warriors, and the Blackwellers up on the battlements could truly see just how vast Dun Scotus's forces in Primley really were.

Abbess Brae's breath caught in her throat at the sight before her. "My Lord, do you mean to capture Blackwell? Because this force is certainly large enough to do so."

"Do not even joke about such a thing, Abbess. If the goodbeasts of the lands supposed for even a moment that I might misuse the power I have amassed, all my work could be undone."

Dun Scotus turned and started down the wall steps. "Come, I will show you that my beasts are, for the most part, honorable ones."

Vondick whispered to Brae as they descended behind the Badger Lord, "Were you joking? About him capturing Blackwell?"

"I'm ... not sure," she replied uncertainly.

It was a large and curious group of Blackwellers that followed Dun Scotus down to the main gate. Old Abbot Graupulous had run down to the archives to fetch Skara and Grauparus, who'd been rounding up records for their wall top reading and were unaware of the events above. Now the three of them joined Brae, Vondick, Gorver, Neo and Woody as part of Blackwell's welcoming committee for Dun Scotus's army. The otter guards unbolted the gate and swung it open so that the Badger Lord and the Blackwell leaders could pass outside for their review of the army. A great many others followed after them, but hung back in the shadows under the wall, reluctant to fully expose themselves to so many armed vermin.

Dun Scotus strode up to the fox who appeared to be the captain, and the squirrel archer standing alongside him. "Your report, Uthalius."

The fox saluted crisply. "Nothing unusual, My Lord. As you can see, we made good time from the north of Primley last night. Full company present, no casualties. We have encountered no foebeasts since the battle with the crows."

"Very good. Tell the troops to stand at ease, and hold here. There is some uncertainty as to where they will be housed."

"Yes, My Lord." Uthalius relayed the order, and immediately the forward fighters relaxed their stance. But no beast broke the neat military ranks within the column.

The Badger War Lord

Abbess Brae and her fellow Blackwellers scrutinized the soldiers, especially the score of foxes near the front. While they no longer stood straight at attention, they kept their gazes directed forward, and did not return the woodlander's curious stares with any of their own, as might have been expected from a gang of unruly vermin. Brae almost felt she was looking at a new kind of creature she'd never seen before. Lord Scotus's "honorable vermin" actually appeared to be a reality, even though she'd not been able to seriously credit the idea before now.

Dun Scotus beckoned for the squirrel and Uthalius to join him where he stood with the Blackwell leaders, just outside the main gate. "Abbess, please allow me to introduce Uthalius the Sword, my Captain of the Guards and Chief of my swordfox brigade." The fox nodded and gave a formal half-bow, but said nothing. "And this is Lady Una, of the Gabbye squirrels. The Gabbye are my most important ally in the Northlands; they have sworn me absolute fealty, and their archery skills are without equal. I could not have enjoyed the success that I have without them."

The gallant squirrel Lady bowed deeply to the Abbess and her companions. Vondick and Woody were riveted by the sight of the proud and powerful Gabbye female; Terious was positive that Lady Una was the most beautiful creature he had ever laid eyes upon.

But the gaze of Brae and the others went quickly back to Uthalius. He was a tall fox, lean and well-muscled, garbed in a black uniform jacket. His only weapon seemed to be the sword slung at his side, but the size of the scabbard hinted at its large size - more than enough to make any woodlander apprehensive.

"Uthalius and Una are my senior officers on this campaign." Lord Scotus motioned toward the open gate. "Let us now go inside, and together we will decide how my forces will be stationed."

Skara began frantically whispering in Brae's ear, not quite so softly that the others could not overhear, "Not the fox! Not the fox!"

Dun Scotus shifted his gaze to the recorder mouse. "Is there some problem?"

Skara stepped forward, drawing himself up to his full height as he addressed the Badger Lord. "Blackwell has suffered greatly at the paws of foxes over the generations.

Why, slaver Salga alone murdered the beloved historian Sutron, for whom one of our bells is named, as well as Blackwell's friar and several others ... not to mention kidnapping some of the Abbey children, including Julien, son of Maximus." Skara turned to the Abbess. "Brae, I do not think we should allow this creature into our home."

Uthalius addressed Brae and Skara directly, in a polite and formal manner. "Those are indeed evil deeds you describe, friend, no doubt committed by an evil beast. But, I am not that fox."

"Please do not presume to call me 'friend' until I know you better," Skara said to Uthalius somewhat frostily.

"Then I hope you will give me the chance for you to do so," Uthalius replied with forced civility.

Dun Scotus looked to Brae. "Abbess, is this the kind of hospitality for which Blackwell is famous?"

"Skara has a point, My Lord. However undiplomatically he may have expressed it. This is a matter that bears some discussion."

"Are foxes in general banned from this Abbey?"

"Well, no ... "

"Then where is the problem? Uthalius is a beast of high honor. He is also my chief captain. I cannot be running outside the Abbey every time I must confer with him. He deserves to be part of our councils. Since you have never met him and do not know him, you have no grounds to exclude him from Blackwell."

Vondick tore his attention away from Lady Una, not at all pleased by the prospect of a fox being invited into his home. As squirrel chief of the Primley Patrol, he'd had to deal with villainous foxes on a number of occasions. "The Abbess decides who enters Blackwell, My Lord, and who doesn't."

Dun Scotus continued as if Vondick had not spoken. "Abbess, you have granted me certain authority in matters of this Abbey's defense. In the name of Blackwell's security, I am saying that Uthalius must be allowed to enter with us. I give you my word of honor as a warrior that he is an honest creature who will cause you no trouble. Now, is he still forbidden to pass through this gate?"

"I never said he was forbidden," Brae said stiffly, "merely that this bore more discussion." She turned to the swordfox. "Friend Uthalius, are you willing to yield your blade to me while you dwell at our Abbey?"

Uthalius hesitated the merest instant, then reached for his weapon. "If those are the rules you have set, then I will abide by them." He drew the sword from its scabbard and presented it to her hilt-first. "Please keep it well. It is most dear to me."

Vondick stepped in front of Brae to spare the Abbess from having to take the heavy sword herself. The squirrel glanced down at what lay in his paw … and then his eyes went wide with amazement. The other Blackwellers around him stared at the blade with jaws agape.

For some moments every beast was struck speechless; then a shadow of anger crossed Vondick's face. "Dun Scotus, is this supposed to be some kind of joke?"

"What do you mean?"

Terious looked to his longtime otter friend. "Show him, Graupuss."

Gorver strode forward, drawing the sword of Septimus from the scabbard at his waist. He held it out alongside the blade Uthalius had presented them.

The two swords were nearly identical!

There were minor differences. The pommel stones were a slightly different shade of red from one another, and the workbeastship of the hilt on the Northlander's sword was some what cruder. But the blade was every bit as keen and splendid as the Blackwell weapon's, not dark and notched like Dun Scotus's sword, but perfect as the day it was forged. Even the point angles and the depth and length of the blood channel seemed identical. If the two of them had not been held side-by-side for comparison, every Abbey beast there could easily have mistaken this new weapon for the cherished sword of Septimus.

Uthalius stood as amazed as any beast. If the fox had suspected that such a near-double of his own weapon was to be found at Blackwell, he was doing a very good job of faking surprise.

"How do you explain this?" Skara demanded of Dun Scotus.

"I did not know that I had to. Did I not tell you, on my very first day at Blackwell, that I had once made a sword very similar to the one Mac Alpine Boar had crafted for Septimus?"

"You did not tell us it was identical!" Brae exclaimed, more flabbergasted than angry. "They are not identical," Dun Scotus calmly pointed out. "Mac Alpine's work is admittedly finer. But then, I crafted Uthalius's sword in a make shift forge in the Northlands, not in the great fires of Astapailia."

"But, why did you copy Septimus's sword?" Brae asked. "The similarity could only be by design."

"It was not."

"But, then how..."

"Who can say what forces speak through a beast who is creating something? I know that the voice of destiny spoke through me when I carved my prophecy into the walls of Astapailia. Perhaps the spirit of Mac Alpine guided my paw as I forged this blade ... just as the spirit of Septimus the Warrior comes to Blackwellers in times of need.

You know I have never been to Blackwell before. I had never set eyes upon that sword, seen a picture of it, or heard any description detailed enough to have recreated it so faithfully. Yet, the similarity is indeed too great to be coincidence. We can only conclude that greater powers are at play here, and leave it at that."

"I suppose ... " Every Blackweller believed in the spirit of Septimus; there was no question in their minds that their founding Warrior watched over them to this day. They accepted Dun Scotus's warning of a dire prophecy without a second thought, for it was well known that the Badger Lords of Astapailia were indeed gifted and cursed with such powers to glimpse the future. Dun Scotus's explanation of the two swords made sense; indeed, there could be no other. There, is proof and a reminder that this badger's existence was not confined to the everyday world of flesh and blood creatures. Only his powers of prophetic vision could account for the sword he had made for Uthalius.

Dun Scotus turned to his fox captain. "Before you accompany us inside, Uthalius, tell the troops they may go around to the south wall and rest there. It may be some time before we reach a decision about which creatures may enter the Abbey, and I would not keep them standing in the road, given how tired they must be from the march. You may as well have Hollnow get started on some sanitation trenches in the meadow there since I'm sure most of the soldiers are in need of relief."

The Blackwellers were taken aback anew. "Uh, Lord Scotus," Brae ventured, "did I just hear you tell Uthalius to issue orders to our Hollnow?"

"Not yours. Mine."

"Do You have your own Hollnow?" Graupulous asked in surprise.

"Naturally. My Tunnel and Trencher Corps of moles has made a difference in more than one of my Northlands battles. Make no mistake, they are trained fighters – every beast who marches with me knows how to handle a weapon - but I prefer to save them from open battle, using their digging skills which are unmatched by any creature. An army of this size must contain more than mere fighting beasts."

Uthalius had already started trotting toward the column to send Dun Scotus's troops around to the south side of the Abbey. Dun Scotus called out after the fox, "Oh, and Uthalius ... tell our newest otter recruit that he may come into Blackwell with us. I am sure the Abbess will have no objections."

"Yes, My Lord." Uthalius issued the orders, and the ranked beasts resumed their forward movement. As the army moved past the Abbey gate on its way to the fields south of Blackwell, an otter who'd stood a few rows back from the lead marchers separated from the column and joined Uthalius as the swordfox strolled back to Dun Scotus and the others.

The otter grinned roguishly and waved at the Abbey leaders in a most unmilitary manner. "Hullo, every beast! Thought it were high time I came back to see how you stodgy Blackwell lot was doin." The graying river beast gestured over his shoulder. "An' as you c'n see, I brought some friends along, harr harr!"

Graupuss almost dropped the sword of Septimus. "Nantuma? Well, thump me rudder! What're you doin' with this crowd?"

Dun Scotus jumped in to explain. "Nantuma has been in my service for nearly a season. He met up with some of my Northlands otters on the far northern fringes of Primley late last spring. No doubt he thought being part of such an army would amount to little more than a chance for adventure for himself ... As you can see, he has yet to master the art of discipline."

Nantuma belatedly stiffened to attention and snapped a sheepish salute to the Badger Lord. "Scot, sorry, M'Lord. Permission to visit with me friends an' family?"

"Permission granted."

No sooner had Nantuma stepped toward the gate than his son Grauparus came bounding out past the Abbess to catch up the grizzled wayfarer in an enthusiastic embrace, right out in the middle of the road. "Dad!"

Many creatures in the still-passing column - rats, shrews, ferrets, stoats, mice, moles and weasels - gave snickering glances toward their embarrassed comrade.

Gorver came up alongside the father-and-son reunion. The otter Skipper shared some of Sister Juliett's opinions about Nantuma's delinquent parenting of his only child, but his heart could not help, but be moved by the joy Grauparus and Nantuma displayed upon seeing each other. "Well, Nany, you've shore gone an' done it this time, bringin' a whole blinkin' army along with you!"

"Had ter, Graupuss matey. They're 'ere t' protect me when Sister 'relia starts wallopin' me skull fer stayin' away so long." Nantuma gave his son a hearty thump on the back that left the younger otter half-winded. "Brady, laddie! Why, ye're almost as big as yer ol' dad! Well, y'do look sharp, an' no mistake - guess Graupuss here's been doin' a good job with you while I've been away. But yer pappy's part of a real regiment now!"

Brae stepped closer to Dun Scotus. "Are you about finished with your surprises, My Lord, or should we expect any more?"

"Yes," added Skara, "after all this, I'm half-expecting to see Septimus the Warrior himself stepping out of your ranks."

"No chance of that, I can assure you," the badger rumbled. "Even though there were times in the north when I would have welcomed his sword and skill, Septimus dwells only here at Blackwell.

As for any other surprises, you will have to wait and see. I know some of you were curious to meet my troops since you could not fully believe in such a thing as noble vermin. Well, now you will have your chance."

Brae and the other Abbey leaders remained in the road by the gate until the last of Dun Scotus's soldiers paraded past and disappeared from view around the southwest corner of the high wall. It would have been impossible to tell how many beasts were in the column, or even how many of each kind there were, although rats and weasels of various types did seem to out number woodlanders by a wide margin, much to the consternation of the Blackwellers. All were well armed.

Brae clasped her paws in front of her, working them nervously. "It will soon be time for lunch. I will tell Friar Calgarus to prepare another special meal for us down in the Great Hall, My Lord, so that Uthalius and Lady Una may dine with us and we may become acquainted."

"Precisely what I would have suggested." Dun Scotus raised a paw toward the gate. "Shall we?"

The curious on lookers farther back quickly cleared the entranceway when they saw the lean, black-clad fox and the armored badger coming their way. Even Lady Una was a creature to give a woodlander pause; with her mighty longbow and full quiver, and no-nonsense expression on her face, it was clear that this Gabbye squirrel could hold her own in any battle.

Inside the Abbey, Vondick made a point of lagging behind the procession.

He discreetly motioned Gorver over to him, whispering loudly, "Get that main gate shut and barred! Listen, make sure all the other wall gates are securely locked, and stay that way. Dun Scotus may insist his vermin are honest and noble, but I'd hate to find out the hard way that they're not ... not with half a thousand of them camped outside our walls!"

"Already on it, Terious matey! My otter lads 'n' lasses were posted at every gate before that rabble even got 'ere. No beast's goin' in or out without our say-so, not even Mr. Red Badger. He c'n keep his soakin' vermin ... noble rats an' foxes me rudder! Don't much fancy th' way they came on us by surprise like that, neither. He knew they were a-comin', an' shoulda told us!"

"I agree," Terious nodded. "My squirrel archers are going to be on the wall top day and night until that horde's gone from here ... and if they think to give us any trouble, they will find out what good shots we are!"

"Still," Graupuss mused, "I reckon we oughtta give him th' benefit of th' doubt, at least until we chat with that fox o' his."

"And Lady Una," added Terious. "I'll be keeping a close eye on her too."

"Oh, I betcher you will!" Graupuss chided with a playful wink. "Keepin' an eye on that proud squirrel maid shouldn't be much of a chore fer you t'all!"

Up ahead, Abbess Brae turned back to the two defenders. "Terious, Graupuss, are you coming? Lord Scotus wants to show his two captains around the Abbey grounds while we're waiting for lunch. I'm sure you will want to join them."

Vondick appraised the situation at paw. Neo stood towering over Uthalius, not even trying to disguise her distrust of the fox, while Woody and several of the other squirrles of the Primley Patrol - all male, he noted - had cemented their attention upon Lady Una. With so much focus on the two newcomers, Terious felt confident that they would not try anything untoward. Not that he'd expect anything like that from a creature as gallant as the squirrel Lady, but the fox was another matter. Hefting Uthalius's sword, Vondick caught up to the others. "Just talking with Graupuss about the weather, wasn't I, matey?"

"Aye, that 'ee was," the otter Skipper corroborated. "Beauty of a day we're havin' t'day, ain't it? Mostly sunny, with a chance o' scattered vermin!"

Young Syril was still in dreamland, even though the sun was nearing its noon tide zenith in the sky over Blackwell.

He'd been up until dawn, standing watch with Vondick. After the shift was over, the squirrel archer went straight down to the Great Hall for the council of Abbey leaders; the Primley Patrol leader was still wide awake, even after the long night of lookout duty.

Syril, however, had never stayed up all night in his life, and was near propping his eyelids open with twigs by the time the eastern sky began to lighten. Only the excitement of their brush with the kite had kept him awake so long, but weariness finally overcame him. When the day shift arrived to relieve them, Syril splashed more cold water onto his face so that he wouldn't fall asleep halfway down the wall steps. Then, he bade Vondick good day, hastened to his room, and climbed into his bed just as his brother Serius was getting up and dressed for the day. Serius thoughtfully draped a blanket over the window to keep the room dark, then hurried down for breakfast even as Syril fell almost instantly asleep. Not even the tollings of the Maximus and Sutron bells to warn of Dun Scotus's approaching army could interrupt the slumbers of the young mouse, as the morning wore on toward noon.

Serius burst into the dormitory room, shouting. "Syril, wake up! There's an army outside!"

Syril opened his eyes and sat up groggily. Serius had intruded upon some dream, the details of which fled from his memory even as he tried to pin them down. In such a state, his brother's excited words made no sense to him whatsoever.

"Huh? What, an army?" Syril pawed at his eyes. "What time is it?"

"Nearly noon. They're gonna have lunch down in the Great Hall, all the Abbey leaders and Lord Scotus..."

Syril shook his head, still not fully awake. "No, that was this morning. He told Vondick last night ... council of leaders, first thing in the morning."

"Well, sure that was during breakfast," said Serius. "But then, when I was down in the archives helping Grauparus and Brother Skara with the records, we heard the bells ringing, and then old Abbot Graupulous came running in to tell us there was a horde coming! You must have heard 'em!"

Syril tried hard to focus on his brother. "What? Heard the horde? What horde?"

"No, the bells! Didn't you hear them?"

Syril ran his paws through his headfur as he sat on the edge of his bed. He really needed a few more hours' sleep.

Serius prattled on. "Brady's dad Nantuma's with them, and then there's a squirrel Lady with a longbow, and a fox with a sword that looks just like the sword of Septimus!"

"Fox? What fox?"

"The one that's down in the Great Hall right now, having lunch with Lord Scotus an' the Abbess an' all the rest. Haven't you been listening to me, Syr?"

Syril stood, pulling on his habit and slipping into his sandals. He didn't have a clue as to what was going on, but Serius was sure excited about something.

"I've been listening, but you're not making any sense."

Serius huffed indignantly. "There is an army outside our walls," he said slowly and simply, as if addressing an infant. "Biggest one anybeast has ever seen. Must be a thousand of 'em - rats, weasels, stoats, ferrets, foxes..."

Syril stared in disbelief. "You mean a genuine, honest-to-goodness horde of vermin has Blackwell under siege?" Syril felt his pulse quicken. "Is Dun Scotus going to help us fight them off?"

"Of course not, silly. It's his army." Serius turned to rush back outside. "You really shouldn't sleep so much, Syr. It makes you muddle-headed."

Chapter 11

It was crowded around the big table in the Great Hall. In addition to Dun Scotus and the eight Abbey leaders - including Strongwing, whose Celtar had seen the army's approach while they were out foraging - there was Uthalius the swordfox and Lady Una the squirrel archer. Brae had also invited Grauparus and Nantuma; their joyous reunion would offset the uneasiness of having a fox in their midst and so many armed vermin outside the walls. Also, Nantuma had spent time in Dun Scotus's service and would provide some insight into that army's activities and, the rogue otter's presence would help keep Dun Scotus, Uthalius and Una honest, in case the Badger Lord and his cohorts were inclined to keep any more surprises from their Blackwell hosts.

Uthalius was carefully seated with Graupuss and Neo at either paw. Without his sword, the fox was probably harmless, but Brae was taking no chances. Either badger or otter would be sure to thoroughly trounce Uthalius in a bare-pawed fight.

Lady Una laid aside her quiver and longbow at the bottom step entrance to the Great Hall, although Brae got the impression that this was done more in observance of proper table etiquette than to put the woodlanders at ease. No beast had asked her to disarm, and perhaps Una felt it only right that, if Uthalius was made to surrender his sword that she would also give up her weapons, at least for the meal.

Terious made a point of placing himself directly across the table from Lady Una. He was normally a very courteous and well-mannered beast, but now he would stare unabashedly at Una for many seconds at a time. Whenever she caught him gazing at her so raptly, he would quickly avert his eyes so as not to appear rude ... but they would soon settle upon her again. Brae noted this visual dance between the two squirrels, then with a smile turned her attention to other matters. With the swordfox sandwiched between Graupuss and Neo, and Terious monitoring Lady Una in his constant manner, the Abbess felt confident that this assembly would not be caught off guard by anything.

Friar Calgarus and his kitchen staff brought down a lunch of hot vegetable pies with leek soup and radish salad. He and his assistants made a show of serving all the food and drink from the side of the table opposite Uthalius, so that they did not have to go near the fox. The normal concerns for keeping up Blackwell hospitality to all guests was no where to be seen in the abrupt manner of the servers.

As Friar Calgarus withdrew from the Great Hall after his final delivery to the table, he was heard to mutter (just loud enough for Uthalius to hear), "Glad I served that apple spice cake this morning ... wouldn't do for such a culinary masterpiece to disappear down the hole of a beast like that."

"Friar, please!" Brae reprimanded him in a loud whisper. "Your manners!"

Friar Calgarus hurried out of the Great Hall with no word of apology and not the slightest hint of contrition on his face. In all honesty, Brae had to admit to herself that she shared at least some of his feelings. But she was Abbess, and she'd granted permission for Uthalius to enter Blackwell as a guest. That meant sharing their food and their table, and treating him as a friend until he proved otherwise.

Uthalius gazed after the mouse Friar. He must have noticed the discourteous behavior toward him, but he seemed totally unperturbed by the incident.

Turning calmly to Brae, he said, "I can see that I am not welcomed by all Blackwellers."

"Please excuse Friar Calgarus. He was a slave during part of his youth, and foxes were to blame."

"It's all right, Abbess. I have learned not to offend easily. I have received such treatment many times in the north, sometimes from the very good beasts I'd just helped. My kind has done much in the past to earn suspicion and distrust from other creatures. I am used to it."

"Yes, he is," agreed Scotus, "although no beast ought to be the object of such scorn. Part of the reason I insisted Uthalius be allowed inside the Abbey was so that you could all get to know him, and come to judge him as an individual, not just as a fox."

"Which is exactly what we're doing here now," said Abbot Graupulous, looking across the table at Uthalius. "I heard Lord Scotus introduce you as 'Uthalius the Sword.' How did you come by such a title? Are you really that good with your weapon?"

"Well ... yes, I am," Uthalius answered earnestly. "But 'Sword' is more of a rank than a title. His Lordship decided many seasons ago that he wanted a brigade of foxes, trained in the use of the broadsword, as his high guard. Since I'd been with Lord Scotus longer than any of my fellow foxes and was the most skilled with my blade, he made me brigade leader and bestowed upon me the special rank of Sword. If I should one day be slain in battle, another fox of the brigade would be promoted to Sword to take my place."

"Very interesting," said Brae, sending a probing stare the fox's way. "I am curious - how long have you been in Lord Scotus's service? And how did the two of you first meet?"

"Oh, it has been ... "Uthalius looked to the badger warrior. "What, My Lord? Over fifteen seasons, unless I am mistaken."

"Seventeen. It was during my first spring in the Northlands, having left Astapailia the previous summer." Dun Scotus expanded his tone to take in every beast at the table. "In those days I traveled mostly alone since that was before I'd begun to assemble my present forces.

One day I came across a small band of foxes, engaged in a fierce fight with a much larger number of searats. I did not know why they were fighting, and so I contented myself to watch for a while, unobserved.

"From my cover, I could see that one fox was mostly responsible for holding the rat enemies at bay. His weapon and style may have been crude, but his skill was undeniable. He'd already ended the lives of several of the searats, and the rest were wary of coming within range of his blade.

But the searat pirates were regrouping for a massed onslaught, and the foxes were sure to be massacred, despite the gallant efforts of their chief swords beast.

Now, I had no great love for either foxes or searats, and might normally have allowed them to inflict as much slaughter upon each other as they could.

But I recognized the makings of a true warrior in the beleaguered swordfox, and could not stand by and watch such potential be destroyed. So, I stepped in and lent my own sword to the side of the foxes. The battle did not last much longer after that."

"And that fox," the Abbess ventured, "was Uthalius?"

"Yes and, he has been with me and served me loyally, from that day to this."

"Did you ever find out what the fight was about?" Graupulous inquired.

Dun Scotus nodded, but gestured for the fox to take up the tale. It was almost as if they had worked out in advance which of them would relate which parts of the tale. Perhaps they'd told it so many times over the seasons that this was an old routine by now.

"We were, I confess, a rather typical band of foxes back in those days," Uthalius said. "My father was our leader. We existed by cheating and conning other beasts, and stealing for our needs whenever mere cheating failed. We weren't killers, although we sometimes had to fight our way out of tight places. That's why my father encouraged me to learn my early sword skills. On this particular day, we had tricked some half-drunk searats out of several kegs of wine and several sacks full of delicacies, plunder which they themselves had only just stolen from far better creatures. We thought we'd got the best of them, but their captain was a vicious sort, and when he learned what had happened to his crewrats, he led a larger force to hunt us down and slay us. We thought we could lose ourselves in the woods, but they had trackers, experienced in the ways of land, which we did not expect. They caught up with us, and we were forced to fight for our very lives." Uthalius raised his cup of ale halfway to his lips. "We didn't really stand a chance. I'd be a dead beast today if Lord Scotus had not come to our rescue."

Vondick could not help speaking quickly into the brief silence. "Of course, if you'd been honest beasts instead of robbers, you never would have had cause to be fighting those rats in the first place."

"Too true," Uthalius readily agreed. "Although I am forced to admit that there was no such thing as an honest fox in the Northlands before Lord Scotus came there. But those rats were savage and violent, and many good beasts as well were murdered or enslaved by them before we encountered them.

132

Had we not been living the lives of decent folk, we might have fared even more poorly against them than we did." Uthalius held up a paw. "Not that I am defending a life of villainy. Those days are long behind me, and I am very glad that they are."

Brae peered over the top of her beaker. "So, you owe Lord Scotus your life."

"Oh, more than that, Abbess. That was merely the first gift he gave me ... and it wouldn't have meant much, if it had been wasted on an ungrateful wretch."

"The sword?"Graupulous asked.

"Well, yes that too, although His Lordship did not forge that for me until he felt I'd earned it." Uthalius ran his gaze around the table, looking steadily into the face of each Blackweller as he spoke. "I know you have all suffered at the paws of foxes in the past, and have good reason to distrust us. It was the same in the north.

My father's band pursued a life of thievery because the good beasts of those lands would never have accepted us into their own midst. We did not even try to be honest or decent since there was nothing for us that way.

"But Lord Scotus changed all that. He believed that goodness could be brought out in nearly every creature. Before the honest folk of the north could be convinced of this, we had to be made to believe it ourselves. He took me, and many other mis-guided beasts like myself, into his service without question or suspicion.

His rules were the same for everybeast under his command: obey his oders, or face punishment. The penalty for out-and-out treachery was death. It was not always easy, especially for foxes and vermin unaccustomed to real discipline.

But Lord Scotus was as quick to reward competence and loyalty as he was to punish disobedience and evil deeds. Those of us who served him well rose through the ranks.

Any advancement in his forces was hard-earned. For the first time in our lives, we were encouraged to feel good about ourselves; a single word of praise from Lord Scotus came to mean more than a hundred stolen meals. The otters and shrews and moles and squirrels and mice who served alongside us began to treat us like brothers in arms, not old enemies and, once they did, so too did the decent good beasts we met on our marches. In just a few short seasons, the bane of many ages was lifted from our existence.

Now could we walk the main paths in the full light of day, heads held high in pride at our new station. It was a strange thing, to suddenly have respect of beasts who had always feared and distrusted us and, now that we have won that respect, we could never go back to the way things were before. I know I speak for every fox in my brigade on this, and for most every rat, weasel, stoat and ferret in the infantry as well. We have been granted a gift greater than any treasure." Uthalius raised his cup high in salute to his badger master. "And we owe it all to Lord Scotus.

I know I have said it many times before, My Lord, but let me repeat it for the benefit of these good Blackwellers: Thank you for what you have given us."

Dun Scotus returned the salute by hoisting his own mug. "It is you who deserves my thanks. The ways of a Badger Lord are hard, mine even harder than most ever since I set out to achieve what many said could never be done. Many better creatures than you were unable to meet the demands of being in my service. You not only outlasted them, but you proved your loyalty and ability in battle time after time, enough to earn promotion to your present high rank. The fox brigade you command keeps order among all the other so-called vermin in my army. I could never have succeeded this far without your hard work.

To you, Uthalius ... may every general have a lieutenant as capable as you."

As Uthalius and Dun Scotus toasted each other, the Blackwellers at the table joined in slowly and uncertainly. A toast given by a fox - or to one - was unheard of down in the Great Hall. It was certainly shaping up to be a day of firsts for Blackwell Abbey.

Abbess Brae said to Uthalius, "So, after Lord Scotus helped you defeat the searats, how did you come to enter his service?"

The fox seemed to hesitate for a heart beat or two.

"He told me a little of his prophecy, and what he hoped to do to bring all creatures together. He said he was impressed by the skill I displayed, and offered to teach me how to better my swordplay if I joined him.

He clearly valued my ability, and a fox does not get such an offer every day.

I jumped at the chance."

"Tell them about your father," Dun Scotus rumbled in an off paw manner.

Uthalius glared at the Badger Lord - an expression not of anger, but of mortification. Lady Una watched her fox comrade, calmly studying him for his reaction.

The awkward silence stretched out as the bewildered Abbeydwellers looked on. From the face Uthalius wore, it was clear that Dun Scotus's casual remark carried some special meaning.

"My Lord, I - "

"Go ahead. Tell these good beasts what you did to your father when he refused to allow you to leave his band of villains to join me."

Uthalius swallowed nervously, gazing around all the expectant faces.

His former swordmaster's confidence seemed to have vanished. At last, looking at no beast in particular, he announced, "I killed him."

The Blackwellers stared horrified at the red fox.

Uthalius slid back his chair and stood. "Please excuse me ... I seem to have lost my appetite." Meeting no gaze, he walked from the table and up the stairs to the Great Hall.

Lady Una was the first to speak after Uthalius had gone.

"Poor Uthalius and, he was trying so hard to make a good first impression."

The squirrel archer turned to Dun Scotus. "Wasn't that a bit cruel, My Lord?"

"I felt it was important for our hosts to know that Uthalius has some dark deeds in his own past. I did not want them to think he was too good to be true."

"Oh, no danger of that," Skara said brusquely.

"Why, that cur!" Gorver opined. "Slayin' 'is own flesh 'n' blood! Only a scallywag who's rotten through an' through could do such a thing."

"Let us not judge Uthalius too harshly," advised Dun Scotus. "Your standards are not those of the savage north, especially back in those days, and especially for villainous creatures. To tell the truth, Uthalius's father was an evil beast who probably would have murdered his own son rather than lose him to me. I might have slain that old one myself, had we met under different circumstances. I believe that villain is much better off dead, and it was the poetic justice of fate that he met his end at the sword of the very beast who otherwise might have followed him down the road of evil."

"Somehow," said Lady Una, "I feel the irony has always been lost on Uthalius. He's carried the knowledge of that deed like a heavy burden for all these seasons. It isn't something he likes other creatures to know about."

This fact was obvious from the way Uthalius had reacted upon being forced to make his admission. Nevertheless, it was hard for any of the Blackwellers to feel much sympathy toward Uthalius - indeed, the whole matter did little to ease their suspicions of the fox in their midst.

"Um, Neo - "Brae caught the badger matriarch's attention, and tried to discreetly signal with her paws that Neo should go after Uthalius, so that the fox would not be free to wander Blackwell unescorted. Unfortunately, it was not easy to be discreet at a crowded table, not with warriors as sharp as Dun Scotus and Lady Una present. After Neo left her seat, Una nodded knowingly.

"Ahh, wise move, Abbess. Honest folk don't want a fox wandering unsupervised among them."

"Sorry - I didn't think I was being so obvious." Brae watched Neo disappear up the steps to the Great Hall, stolidly chasing after Uthalius. "But I can't say this little tale about Uthalius and his father has done much to cheer us up. I suppose there's nothing to be concerned about, really, but ... old habits, you know."

"Oh, we know exactly how you feel," Una assured the Abbess. "I've had to put a shaft into many a fox during my seasons, even after I learned to regard Uthalius as a true friend. You've nothing to fear from that fox, but there are still many others of his kind who are evil to the core. Far better to risk offending an honest beast than to trust too easily, and pay with your lives."

The squirrel Lady spoke with a more carefree confidence than either Dun Scotus or Uthalius, as if nothing in the world could bother her. The Blackwellers found themselves immediately liking her, except for Vondick; enchanted was the only word to describe how he felt about his fellow squirrel from the far north.

"And what about you, Lady Una?" Brae asked. "How did you come to be in the service of Lord Scotus?"

"In his service?" Una took a long quaff of ginger-spiced ale. "A rather inaccurate choice of words, Mother Abbess. While I take orders from Lord Scotus, I am not truly one of his soldiers. The Gabbye are more allies to his Lordship than members of his army."

"But, you have sworn him fealty?"

"As a tribe, yes. But we have our own chain of command, which we follow even when we fight alongside Lord Scotus. So, while we will respond to any request for assistance that he makes of us and obey his orders on the field of battle, we lie outside his main forces. That is one reason why I am the only Gabbye squirrel to travel with him to Blackwell: I am more of an envoy than a soldier in this army. Also, Blackwell has very special meaning to us, and I have come to address that as well."

The Abbess was quite surprised. "You know of Blackwell, so far north?"

"Indeed we do and, before I explain further, perhaps I should ask how much you know of us?"

Brae deferred to Skara, who knew more than any Blackweller about such matters.

"Yes, I've been dying to ask you," the recorder mouse began, "are you the same Gabbye who aided Septimus the Warrior in the Battle of Bramwall, more seasons ago than Blackwell has been standing?"

Lady Una nodded. "Just as you are the same Blackwellers who have dwelt in this fine Abbey since Septimus and Abbess Grethin built it. More so, probably, since we can trace a director ancestor back to those ancient times. Tell me, what do you know of Blackwell's first squirrel archer, Lady Susan, or her family?"

"Um ... I recognize the name of Lady Susan," Skara said, searching his memories of his archive readings. "She is mentioned numerous times in the chronicles of the Wildcat War, which Septimus and the good beasts of Primley fought before Blackwell was built. But I do not know anything about any other members of her family."

"She had a son." Una glanced across the table to meet the gaze of the Blackwell squirrel chief who was so attentive to her. "A son named Vondick."

This revelation brought raised eyebrows and surprised chuckles from around the table. Graupuss winked at his old squirrel friend. "Hear that, Terious matey? Ye're ancient!"

"Did Vondick play some part in Blackwell history of which we should be aware?" Skara inquired.

"Not exactly Blackwell history," Una answered. "I am not surprised that his name is unknown to you, although he was born here at this Abbey. Your warrior Septimus was an old mouse by the time Vondick was nearing adulthood. It is spoken among the Gabbye that Septimus saw in the young squirrel a fierce and restless warrior's spirit that reminded him of his own youth. Although Septimus had sworn never to speak of his tragic past in the Northlands to any beast of Primley, he made an exception for his friend Helga's son - not the entire story, but just enough to let Vondick know that there was a whole forest full of wild, aggressive squirrels in the far north, squirrels in need of taming and a real leader if they ever hoped to have a place among decent creatures.

"As you can imagine, Vondick's soul was fired by this tale. He knew he must go to that very same forest that Septimus had visited in his youth, to find those squirrels and tame them. We were the Gabbye, so savage and violent that most creatures regarded us as enemies, even after we had helped Septimus fight the Battle of Bramwall and rid the east coast of the slaver tyrant. When, after several seasons of traveling, Vondick finally stood at the brink of our domain and gazed upon us, he cannot have liked what he saw.

"But he was equal to the challenge. Like Septimus the Warrior, he would not be daunted by a difficult task, nor would he shy away from what needed to be done. He challenged our vicious chieftain Ramaldy for leadership of our tribe, and slew Ramaldy in single combat to the death. In the next season's time, Vondick had to slay two others who sought to make themselves chieftain. Thanks to the training Vondick had been given by Septimus, no other squirrel was able to best him, and after those two attempts none tried.

"Vondick took a mate, marrying into the Gabbye and making our forest his home forever more. It was then that he set upon his greatest task: to turn these wild squirrels he had found into decent, respectable, skilled fighters who would be both friend and ally to all other good beasts of the Northlands. Now, he was unbeatable in paw-to-paw combat, but Vondick's archery skills, learned from his mother Lady Helga, were even more formidable. No beast of any kind in all the north could fly a shaft as long and true as he could, and it was this skill that he undertook to teach all the Gabbye.

"He was a good teacher, and a great leader. By the time he grew too old to be chieftain any longer, he had a fine, strong son to take his place. From that day to this, the Gabbye have always been ruled by a direct descendant of Vondick's.
My brother Mallnus and I can trace our lineage straight back to him, and thence to Lady Helga of Primley. So, in a sense, we are Blackwellers."
"Well, shiver me whiskers an' stomp me rudder!" Graupuss declared. "Now that's more the kind o' story we Blackwellers like t' hear. Shore beats that nasty ol' fox slaying 'is nasty ol' father."
"Yes," said the Abbess, "it's good to know that the spirit of Blackwell survives in far away lands as well as in our own Abbey. But, I am very surprised we never heard of any of this before."
"Well, Vondick left Blackwell when he was quite young, and never returned in all his days," said Una. "His great deeds were done in a land where the creatures of Primley never ventured and, even after he died and his legend began to grow among our tribe, his descendants were kept too occupied by constant war and strife to send word of all that had happened back to Blackwell. From the viewpoint of your own histories, he would have seemed nothing more than a young wanderer who one day set out for adventure and was never heard from again. Hardly the stuff of Blackwell legend, even if his mother was Lady Helga. But you can see why I was very surprised to find that you had a squirrel named Vondick living at the Abbey today.
It is almost like a token of fate that these are indeed times of destiny, when I can travel to Blackwell and find the namesake of our tribe's founder living here to greet me."
"And so our history grows." Skara had produced some loose sheets of paper and an ink-filled stylus from within his habit, and now set about furiously scribbling at his place, food and drink pushed aside for the moment. Forgetting all aspects of proper table etiquette, he was intent only upon capturing as many of the Gabbye squirrel's words as he could while her tale was still fresh in his memory. "I will want to speak with you more later, at your convenience, My Lady.
This is an important part of our history of which we were unaware, and it should be entered into the chronicles in as much detail as you can provide."
"Oh, there will be plenty of time for that," Una assured him. "I expect to be around for some time."

Vondick, staring across the table at his fellow squirrel, felt his heart quicken with hope. "M'Lady, are you planning to stay here at Blackwell, as a permanent member of our community? If so, you would be most welcome."

The male squirrel's attentions toward her had not been lost on Lady Una. Almost coyly, she said to Vondick, "Oh, I've no doubt of that. I could have guessed that without you having to say a word."

Terious self-consciously cleared his throat and looked down at his plate, ears reddening slightly. But within moments his gaze was firmly back on Una; he could not keep his eyes off her for very long.

Una addressed Brae and the others. "Lord Scotus has discussed with us the idea of bringing some of the Gabbye south to help with the defense of Primley in its times of need. So far, we have seen nothing on this march to suggest you folk are in any immediate jeopardy, but things change. If this plan is put into effect, it would make sense for one of the Gabbye leaders to relocate to Primley in order to over see our forces here.

Most likely, my brother Mallnus, who is the chieftain of the Gabbye, would remain in the north, where his warrior's skills and leadership are most needed, and I would come to these fair lands as the Gabbye commander in the south. All this depends, of course, upon what the days ahead bring."

"Why do you say that?" the Abbess asked.

Dun Scotus took over from Lady Una. "I had three purposes in coming here.

The first was to share my prophecy with the leaders of Blackwell, and help improve this Abbey's defenses in any way that I could. This I have done. My second aim was to travel throughout much of Primley country, to gauge the temper of the woodlands and judge for myself if any trouble loomed near. We have found none so far, but my army has only been north of Blackwell, and there is still a great expanse of forest to the south that I wish to investigate. I will have the opportunity to do so when I set out to achieve my third objective."

"Which is?" Graupulous asked.

"To go to Astapailia. I have not spoken with my brother Nantrom in many seasons, and the time has come for the two of us to work together as one. I do not know whether I will reclaim the throne of the mountain and make Atapailia my permanent home once more, or return to the Northlands to continue my work there while my brother guards the coastlands.

It will all depend upon what I find when I get there, and whether I encounter any trouble along the way. I would like to give my troops a few days' rest here at Blackwell, then we will depart."

"Soooo ..." Brae ventured, "you will only be staying with us for several days more?"

"My stay at Blackwell was never meant to be more than temporary. I have much to do elsewhere, and although I would dearly love to remain here longer, I cannot. I also realize that the number of my troops is a strain on your Abbey, and I would not impose upon you any longer than necessary."

"Well ... anything we can do to help speed you on your way, simply let us know."

Brae hoped she didn't sound too eager. But every Blackweller at the table shared her sense of relief that Dun Scotus's horde of vermin would soon be on its way.

Chapter 12

Burr hurr, oi never berlieved thurr wurr so many vermin in th' whole wurld!
Rufus the mole stood upon the south ramparts, flanked on either paw by Syril and
Serius. He and the mouse brothers were equally captivated by the sight of Dun
Scotus's army, spread out on the meadow beyond the south wall.

"They're all mixed up together, all kinds of creatures," Serius exclaimed, pointing from
place to place among the resting troops. "Look over there, there's a whole squad
of otters, more'n we have in all of Blackwell. An' they're talking and laughing with
a bunch o' weasels like they're old friends and, down there are scores of shrews, all
mixed in with scores more o' rats. An' I see ferrets, an' hedgehogs - "

Young Rufus pushed his spiny head between them. "Hogs? Where? Where?"

" - and even some mice, just like us, Syr!"

"Yurr hurr, an' thurr be sum molers, just loik oi!" Rufus said excitedly.

Syril was as excited as any of them, but his amazement held him silent for the
moment. Vermin and good beasts, all tossed together like the makings of an otters'
hotroot stew! It was like the world had suddenly been turned topsy-turvy, with all
the old, accepted ways stood on their head.

If he weren't seeing it with his own eyes, Syril wouldn't have believed it.

Even now, with the sight laid out below him on the sun-drenched pasture, he wasn't sure he believed it.

There was one group in Dun Scotus's army that didn't mingle with the rest, holding itself apart most conspicuously. Syril's eye was drawn to their neat black uniforms and the large swords that hung at their sides. "Those foxes don't seem too friendly with the others," he observed.

Ularus the cellar keeper was one of the many adult Blackwellers up on the battlements along with the youngsters, pacing back and forth as they warily monitored the armed beasts outside. "No surprise there, Syril lad. No beast likes bein' round them scoundrels, not even their fellow vermin. Rat's 'n' weasels're bad 'nuff, but foxes're the worst o' the lot!"

Syril felt he had to agree. Every Blackweller knew of the treachery of Slagar during the time of Maximus the Second Warrior and, then there was the trouble caused by the Marlfoxes a few generations later. And, of course, their very own Friar Calgarus had been enslaved by foxes in his youth. It would be hard to find an Abbeydweller who would argue Ularus's point. Foxes were definitely the worst and, now there was a score of them here at Blackwell.

"Their leader went down to the Great Hall to meet with the Mother Abbess," Serius said. "Vondick took his sword first ... they say it's just like Septimus's!"

"Aye, that's true," Ularus nodded, "I was there an' saw it my own self. An exact copy, or close 'nuff to fool these eyes. How a dirty fox got t' have his stinkin' paws on a weapon that fine I'll never fathom. But it ain't right!"

Woody the squirrel leaned against the wall top close by. "Prob'ly got it the same way he got his high rank: Dun Scotus gave it to him. What that badger's all about is beyond me." He glanced out over the meadow below. "Something strange ... not a single squirrel in all that horde, 'cept for the one who is down in the Great Hall right now. Wonder why that is?"

The young otter Harden lounged next to Woody. "No mystery there. That band o' foxes has enough bushy tails for this whole army!"

Harden was dividing his attention between the meadow outside and the Abbey grounds. He and his fellow otters were in charge of guarding the wall gates, to make sure no beast tried to open them from within or without.

He suddenly stiffened to attention when he saw Uthalius, alone and unsupervised, emerge onto the lawns from within the Abbey.

"Hey, lookout there!" he called to the others around him. "Wot's that fox doin' down there all by himself?"

Every beast turned to look. Harden's grip tightened on his javelin, while Woody automatically notched an arrow to his bowstring.

"That's not good," the squirrel said ominously. "The elders would never have let him leave the Great Hall without an escort - "

Even as Woody spoke, Neo followed Uthalius out onto the grounds. The Abbey-dwellers atop the wall all heaved a collective sigh of relief.

"Well, that's more like it," Harden said. "Neo can handle any grief that fox dishes out. Still, suppose we'd better keep an eagle eye on 'em, just in case."

While the young otter kept up his vigil, the others returned their attention to the mighty horde outside the wall.

Neo almost ran into Uthalius in her haste to catch up with the fox. Uthalius had his back to her, so she was able to slow, to a normal walk before he turned at the sound of her approach. She ran up the stairs and through the Great Hall left her panting in the summer heat, betraying the fact that she'd been chasing after him. Like Abbess Brae, Neo didn't want to appear too obvious that this particular guest of Blackwell was not trusted enough to be left on his own.

Uthalius turned to greet her with a scowl on his features. But he quickly chased it away with a look of chagrin and embarrassment.

"Sorry. As a captain of the guard, I'm not used to being guarded myself."

"Oh ... er, it's not that," Neo stammered untruthfully. "It's just that it's not our custom to allow guests to wander about without a guide their first day here." She didn't know why all of a sudden she should care what this creature though about her ... but she did.

"You are too courteous. I'm going back out to rejoin my troops. I would like my sword back, please."

"Oh, the Abbess had it put up in her private study so that no beast would toy with it. I couldn't go in there alone without permission."

"I was given to understand I would only have to surrender my weapon while I was inside Blackwell. I can't appear before my beasts stripped of my sword. It is my symbol of rank and honor."

"Well, then, don't go outside." Neo gestured toward the orchard. "Let's go sit where it's cool. If you still feel like leaving the Abbey when lunch is over down at the Great Hall, Brae can get your sword for you then."

Uthalius studied the badger before him. "After what I said down there, I wouldn't have thought any of you would want to be around me if you didn't have to."

Neo chose her words before speaking. "I don't know you, Uthalius. But I've had enough time to get to know Lord Scotus to be sure of one thing: you would not be a captain in his army if you were a truly evil beast."

"Yes, but sometimes even good beasts can commit evil deeds."

Neo nodded. "If they are truly good beasts, they can put their past misdeeds behind them and get on with living decent lives."

The fox gave her an assessing look. "Most creatures would not be so understanding about what I did."

"Most creatures are not Blackwellers," Neo shot back. "Lord Scotus said your father probably deserved his fate. I was not there, so I will not judge you, however tempted, I might be. I can only tell you that you are not acting like an evil beast, who would feel no remorse over such a thing and might even go so far as to brag about it. You obviously do not feel that way. You seem ashamed of your deed, as any good-hearted creature would."

Uthalius shrugged and glanced away. "Perhaps my father did deserve such a fate. But I take no pride that it was I who made him meet it." He looked toward the orchard. "Now that you mention it, the shade under those trees do look inviting. I can rejoin my troops later. Would you care to join me?"

"Of course." Neo escorted Uthalius over to the fruit grove, where the pawful of Abbeydwellers lunching there would surely be surprised to find a fox suddenly in their midst. "Perhaps your appetite has returned enough to sample some more of our tasty fare. There's always plenty for every beast."

Neo studied Uthalius out of the corner of her eye as she walked alongside him. An honorable fox? Maybe.

Or maybe, Neo thought to herself, you are merely a very good actor, my friend. She would not let this one out of her sight, not while he dwelt within Blackwell's peaceful grounds.

Friar Calgarus and Brother Marko stood upon the ramparts along with most of the other Abbeydwellers, regarding the massed force of mixed creatures arrayed out in the south meadow. Even a few of the Celtar had joined the onlookers, hopping sure-clawed along the crenellated wall top. Bird and beast alike continued to engage in speculation over what it all meant.

The two mice most responsible for feeding the Abbey had more than just idle speculation on their minds, however.

Marko turned to the Friar, whiskers wrinkled in worry. "You don't suppose they will all be staying, do you? Inside Blackwell, I mean?"

"Inside or out, they will be our guests if the Abbess says they are," Hugh replied gruffly. "And from what I caught of the conversation down in the Great Hall, my guess is they will be around for a while." The Friar was clearly none too pleased by this prospect.

"But ... the storm!" the horticulturalist mouse fretted, wringing the frayed ends of his habit cord. "We lost so much of the harvest! We'd have enough hardship feeding so many hungry mouths even in the best of times. But now, I don't see how there will possibly be enough food to go around!"

"Nor do I," Friar Calgarus agreed. "Not without putting our stocks so low that we'd starve over the winter." He glanced toward the orchard, where Uthalius had been seen to go with Neo a short time before. "Well, I'm not about to see a single Black-weller go hungry, just so we can feed the likes of that."

"You are one hundred percent right, so far as those villainous vermin go. But what about Lantron's other troops? He's got otters, shrews, moles, hedgehogs, even other mice ... we can't turn them down if they ask to be fed. And how can we give food to some without giving it to all?"

"Very easily," Calgarus answered. "Allow only the decent creatures inside, and keep the rabble out. They can fend for themselves in the woods, and that way we'll know that none of our precious food is being wasted on beasts who don't deserve it!"

Brother Marko shook his head. "You've got it all figured out. But if the Abbess says otherwise, we will still have to abide by her wishes. If that means feeding every beast in that army, then we will."

"Why would she do something that would endanger the health of decent wood-landers? She can't, and that's all there is to it. You and I will simply have to make it clear to her that there's not enough food to go around, and help her come to the right decision. After all, we're the ones who have to keep Blackwell fed, not her."

There was something mutinous in the Friar's tone, and Marko wasn't sure he cared for it. "But she's the Abbess ... "

"Yes, she is," said Calgarus. "This means she must do what is best for Blackwell. For that, she must heed the advice of every beast who help run this Abbey. If she should happen to forget that this is her place, it's up to us to remind her, and advise her what is best ... for Blackwell, not for some gang of unruly vermin camped outside our walls."

Marko cast an eye down to the meadow. Dun Scotus's army was neither unruly nor, as he'd pointed out, all vermin. "Yes," he agreed hesitantly, "certainly we must advise her. But I'm not sure I like your tone..."

The Friar gave an indignant snort. "You've never been a slave, have you? Well, I have ... and, it was the likes of those down there who put me in chains and kept me there for two seasons of my youth. Boils my blood, just knowing that fox weaseled his way into a lunch down in the Great Hall with our leaders."

Brother Marko scratched at his snout, reluctant to enter a full-blown argument with Calgarus. "Well, the Abbess could have chosen to make the fox stay outside, but she didn't. Maybe we're forgetting what Blackwell is all about."

"It's not about us going hungry because we had to feed some army we never invited here."

Marko glanced toward the main Abbey. "Oh, look, the meeting seems to have let out. Here, comes Gorver, and Vondick, and Dun Scotus with that squirrel Lady. Don't see the others, though. They must still be inside."

Graupuss headed out to the orchard, but Vondick made straight for the wall steps, bounding up them to the high walkway. He dodged past the two mice and a dozen other Blackwellers until he got to Woody. The onlookers pressed close to hear what their squirrel arms master had to say.

"Hey, stand back a bit, give us some room!" he called out, then turned to his second-in-command. "Woody, pass the word to all the Primley Patrol, and to all the otters too. The Abbess has called a private meeting of just the main Abbey leaders, up in her study. We'll need Neo there too, so it's up to you to keep a sharp eye on that fox as long as he's inside our walls. Oh, and keep this kinda mum ... we're doing this on the sly from Lord Scotus. The Abbess told him we'll be meeting about routine Abbey business."

"Ur, don't you think he will be able to figure out on his own what you're up to?"

"Probably. But Brae doesn't want to be too blatant about it."

"Okay. You can count on us," Woody assured Terious, with a half-salute.

Vondick turned to head backdown the stairs, but Friar Calgarus caught his sleeve as he passed. "I'd like to be there too. If this is about that army staying at Blackwell, I've got some things to say about that."

"Sorry, Friar, but it's going to be pretty crowded up in that study. There'll be time later for you to bend Brae's ear about anything you want."

Calgarus started to insist, but Terious was already gone, flashing down the wall steps to rejoin the other Abbey leaders.

"Well, I never," the Friar huffed. "No more acorn crunch surprise for that squirrel this season! Speaking of which, I'd better go and get a start on the evening meal, now that lunch is more or less finished." He started down the stone stairway, following in Vondick's wake at a far more sedate and dignified pace. "Though it sure would help," he grumbled to himself, "if I knew how many beasts I'll be cooking for!"

Vondick was right: the study of Abbess Brae was quite crowded, and the situation wasn't helped any by Neo's return.

"Sorry for the holdup," she apologized, squeezing into the room between Gorver and Hollnow and securing the door behind her. "I gave Uthalius his sword back, and escorted him outside. Lord Scotus and Lady Una went with him. Dun Scotus's going to give his troops a formal review. He was strongly hinting that he wanted some of us to join him."

"And so we will," said Brae, "as soon as we're finished here."

"Glad he didn't press the point; we would have had a hard time explaining what matters are more important than what's to be done about his army."

"Well, that's what we're here to discuss. Amongst ourselves, not with Lord Scotus." Brae ran her gaze around the chamber; in addition to herself, Neo, Graupuss and Hollnow, also present were Graupulous, Vondick, Skara and Strongwing. Only Arlyn, in deference to his age, was allowed the privilege of a soft high backed chair, while the Celtar leader perched above him. Every beast else stood.

The badger matriarch leaned her bulk against the door; like most of the doors in Blackwell, this one could not be locked without a key, and the Abbess didn't want this meeting disturbed by any beast who hadn't been invited.

"I can see these quarters are rather close for so many of us, and since Lord Scotus is waiting for us, I'll keep this as brief as I can," the Abbess began. "An army has come to our home, an army composed largely of creatures who have traditionally been our enemies. Dun Scotus says that they are honest and trustworthy and, maybe they are. But I cannot take his word for this. I am Abbess, and if even one Blackweller loses its life to this army that death will be on my head. I will not let that horde inside this Abbey. Not yet, anyway."

She studied the faces of her friends, and did not see a single look of disagreement among them. "Dun Scotus says he wants us to get to know his beasts and judge them for ourselves. We will certainly take him up on his offer ... starting with that fox Uthalius. Neo, you've already spent some time alone with him. Well, you're going to spend a lot more. You and Uthalius are about to become inseparable friends ... or at the least, inseparable. I want you by his side his every waking moment that he's within our walls, not just to guard him, but to study him. If there's something rotten about him, he will slip and let it show sooner or later."

Neo grimaced. Even though she'd found her visit with Uthalius in the orchard not at all unpleasant, she did not relish the thought of being glued to him like an oarslave aboard a pirate ship.

"You can count on me, Brae. I won't let him out of my sight."

"Very good." She turned to her squirrel friend. "Terious, I'm sure you will find your assignment more agreeable than Neo's. Dun Scotus only has one squirrel in his present army, but she seems an important part of his force. It was, um, rather obvious all through lunch that you've taken quite a shine to Lady Una, and I'm sure you're hoping to spend a lot of time with her. Well, you will. I don't know if you can capture her fancy as much as she's captured yours, but you will have plenty of opportunity to find out.

Talk to her, Terious, for as many hours as she can stand. Get her to open up to you. Find out everything you can about the Gabbye and their real relationship with Lord Scotus, what conditions are like these days in the Northlands, and her experiences during her service with him. Try your best to stay impartial, however smitten you become, so you can gauge whether she's being truthful. I doubt a squirrel is as likely to lie as a fox, but we must take nothing for granted. Pay close attention to all that she tells you, and be on guard for discrepencies and contradictions in her tales. Also, be alert to things she might try to hide or answers that are evasive. Dun Scotus was less than forth-coming to us about having vermin in his army, and having such a large force so close to Blackwell. Perhaps his captains practice such deception as well."

Vondick nodded, although honestly it was difficult for him to believe that any creature as strong and proud - yes, and beautiful - as Lady Una could be playing them false. "I'll try my best ... and I'm sure I'll have a lot of volunteer help from the other squirrels of the Primley Patrol. The males, anyway. But, what about that story she told of the other Vondick and Lady Helga? Do you really think the whole thing could have been made up?"

"I don't know."Brae looked to the historian in their midst. "Skara, you say you don't recall any mention of Helga's son in the early records at all?"

Skara still clutched at the notes hurriedly made his way down towards the Great Hall from Una's tale. "No, it was all new to me. I suppose I could do a more careful search for such details, now that all the early chronicles are out and easily at paw anyway..."

"If you could, please. Although if those events really did happen as she told us, she's probably right about no beast at Blackwell making note of it. Your present search for clues to Dun Scotus's prophecy is your most important task at the moment ... and, today's events may even help you. I cannot believe that such a horde as that which has come to us today was not foreseen by one of our ancestors. Look for references to great numbers of beasts coming here, especially vermin and woodlanders together."

"I've been through all the early records most carefully, and I don't recall any such thing." Skara shrugged. "But, I'll look again. Maybe I missed it, or maybe there will be something about it in one of the later histories I haven't gotten to yet. But you're right: it does give us more to go on than we had."

Brae looked to Gorver. "Back to the matters at paw. There are a lot of otters in Dun Scotus's army outside. Graupuss, I want you and all of your otters to mingle with your brethren from the north. No beasts are more outgoing than otters, and I'm sure an entire squad of them could never hold a secret or keep up a lie for very long ... especially from other otters. Be friendly, and just let them talk as they will. But pay very close attention, just as I told Terious to do with Lady Una.

"Of course, there is one otter among them in particular who might be able to tell us the most. Cozy up to Nantuma. He's a Blackweller, or at least his son is, and he's only been with Dun Scotus for a season. His first allegiance will be to us. I doubt he could have been kept in the dark for an entire season with Dun Scotus's otters; I'm relying on him to tell us if there's anything afoot we should know about. He will be spending a lot of time with Grauparus, Graupuss, so that will give you a good reason to hang about with both of them since you've been like a second father to Brady.

Find out everything you can, and report to me, Neo or Terious at once if something out of sorts does pop up."

The otter Skipper saluted his Abbess. "Aye, Neo! Me an' me lads 'n' lasses'll politely twist some flippers 'mongst Dun Scotus's otters. Won't any secret keep from us while I'm at th' helm! An' I'll knock heads with Nantuma personally. Never been favorites with each other, mind, but I'll make good 'n' shore we get along smooth as hazel brandy this time."

"I'm sure you will do a fine job." Brae nodded toward Hollnow. "I guess I hardly have to tell you what your assignment is, Hollnow. Dun Scotus has an entire corps of moles out there. While Graupuss and his otters are making fast friends with Dun Scotus's otters, you will be doing the same with his moles. Just ask them about moleish things what their place is in Dun Scotus's army, how their skills are used, the experiences they've had under his command.

Make it look like you are simply comparing your own tunneling and building past times to theirs, and let come out in their stories whatever may. Show their Hollnow around Blackwell if you wish; this Abbey was largely built by mole skills, and the mere sight of what we have here should be enough to impress any Northlander who's never seen such a place."

"Yurr hurr, et's roight 'nuff thurr, marm. Oi'll do moi bestest."

Brae drew a deep breath. "Which leaves all the scores of rats, stoats, weasels and ferrets. We don't have any of those of our own. But Neo thinks we've been invited to review Dun Scotus's troops, and I think that's a fine idea. So before any of you set about the tasks I've just given you, let's have a closer look at this army as a whole. Graupuss, Terious, you will join me in this. You too, Neo. This will be our rule from now on: no beast allowed outside the wall unless you're armed and in groups. Lord Scotus has made a point of showing us several times how he feels our vigilance should be improved. We'll be very vigilant now."

"Do I understand," Skara asked the Abbess, "that you plan on going out there yourself to meet that army? I don't think that's a very good idea, Brae."

"I agree," seconded old Abbot Graupulous. "It's too risky."

"How else are we going to find out what we need to know?" Brae challenged.

"You're too valuable to risk," Graupulous said. "Let me go in your stead. I was Abbot once, after all, so Dun Scotus should accept my authority nearly as much as yours and, if anything untoward does occur, well, I can be spared. You cannot."

Brae was about to protest, then relented. "Are you sure this is something you're willing to do, Graupulous?"

"I'll have Graupuss, Neo and Terious to guard me. That should be safe guard enough."

"Aye," the otter nodded, "an' I'll bring Brady along too. He's young, but he can handle a javelin better'n most beasts twice 'is age. Nantuma might lend a paw too, if trouble breaks out."

"And my squirrels will be watching closely from the ramparts," Terious added. "They're very good shots."

"And I'd like to join them too," Strongwing chimed in. "I'll be in no danger since I can fly away at the first sign of trouble. To rally my Celtar, of course," he hastily added, not wanting to look like he was thinking only of his own welfare.

"All right," Brae nodded her acceptance. "See if you can seek out the vermin captains first. Between the five of you, you should be able to tell whether they are dangerous and if it would be safe for me to meet them myself. Just be careful, all of you. Keep on your toes. Keep your eyes and ears open.

If there is danger at our door, I'd like to know it before any Blackwellers come to harm. At the very first sign that those 'honorable vermin' are not what Dun Scotus says they are, he and his horde will find themselves locked outside our walls and told to move on."

"Easier said than done," Skara remarked. "I get the feeling that Dun Scotus doesn't take orders from any beast, not even the Abbess of Blackwell."

"Unless he wants his name to be reviled by every good beast in Primley, he will honor our wishes," Brae said firmly.

"And if he doesn't care whether his name is reviled?" asked Skara.

"Then let's go find out what kind of badger this is who's come to us. You all know what to do. Let's get to it and, be careful, my friends."

Every beast filed out of the study, until Brae was left alone with Graupulous. Abbess and former Abbot looked at each other across Brae's desk.

"I was listening to myself just now," she sighed, "and I can't believe I'm saying such things about a Badger Lord of Astapailia. A guest of our Abbey, who's come to warn us of a crisis and offer us his help ... "

"Who, as you pointed out yourself, has kept things hidden from us," Graupulous responded. "And who has brought this army here without warning, even after we'd asked him to give us notice so we would have time to prepare. He was talking to a kite of his last night; he must have known how close his force was to Blackwell. In, fact I'd wager my whiskers that was when he gave the order for them to march on us today. Rather, under-pawed behavior, if you ask me, and not at all what I'd expect from a Badger Lord."

"He'd just say he was trying to prove a point - that a large army could approach Blackwell without us being aware of it and, now he will want to cut down those trees. Terious will have a fit!"

Graupulous smiled. "I do believe our Vondick is so distracted by Lady Una that Dun Scotus could cut down half the trees in Primley and that squirrel wouldn't notice! But, Dun Scotus has given us no choice. His own deeds demand that we treat him with suspicion, at least as long as he has so many armed rats and weasels and foxes outside our gates."

Brae sighed deeply. "Whenever Blackwell faced an enemy in the past, we knew we were dealing with creatures of pure evil. What are we facing now? I cannot believe a Badger Lord would be our foe, and yet he is not acting fully like a friend either. It is a quandary."

"Perhaps he is neither one," Graupulous said slowly. "Friend or foe, I mean. It's that dire prophecy of his. He's got his own agenda, and he's going to do whatever he will, regardless of what we or any beast else thinks about him."

"You may be right," Brae agreed. "Any creature touched by the powers of fate so strongly as he has been must perhaps follow a path apart from all others. If that is true, I cannot imagine what a lonely and grim existence it must be for him."

"There is that," admitted Graupulous. "It's certain that no beast has ever done any-thing at all like he's done ... no creature but a Badger Lord could possibly have pulled it off. Maybe no beast with evil intent could keep that force together."

"But just because it can be done, doesn't make doing it a good idea. I'm not ready to give Dun Scotus my sympathies just yet, no matter how cheerless a life he'd led. That's his affair; those vermin and foxes outside are ours, and he's got no right to let them loose in Primley if they are bound to do harm." Brae gazed searchingly at her mentor. "I'm beginning to have second thoughts about letting all of you go out there. What if something does go wrong? Most of the Abbey leadership would be wiped out."

Graupulous shrugged. "I still think it's better to find out this way than to remain in the dark. You and Skara will be staying inside, and I couldn't think of better paws in which to leave Blackwell. Woody is an admirable lieutenant of the Forest Patrol, and would make a formidable commander in Vondick's absence and, don't forget Hollnow. Not to mention Friar Calgarus, and Sister Juliett, and Brother Marko ... "

"And young Syril," Brae added with a grin, "our newest Abbey champion!"

"Oh, yes, we mustn't leave him out! So you see, Brae, even if the worst should happen out there today, Blackwell will still be left with strong leadership. But I'm betting that nothing will happen. If Dun Scotus had wanted to take this Abbey, he could have done it before now and, if he doesn't, then he'd have no reason to let us come to harm. I do think he sincerely wants to remain in our good graces, whatever his motives might be."

"Even if that's true," said Brae, "what of all those vermin? You and the others will be walking right into an army of them. Can they be trusted not to cause you any harm?"

"Dun Scotus would seem to think so and, if he's really trying to make a good impression with us, I'd guess that it will be woe to anybeast in his forces who so much as musses our fur."

"I hope you're right, Graupulous, my dear old mouse."

"So do I, Brae. So do I." The retired Abbot rose gingerly from his chair. "But I won't find out just sitting here, gathering dust. Let's have a close look at these vermin for ourselves and, then we will see what we will see."

(To be continued in The Badger War Lord, Book II: Armies)

www.ingramcontent.com/pod-product-compliance
Lightning Source LLC
Chambersburg PA
CBHW070808050426
42452CB00011B/1952